How to Analyse Poetry

Art of Poetry

Volume one

Neil Bowen

Matthew Curry, Michael Meally & Sally Rowley

Published by pushmepress.com an imprint of Inducit Learning Ltd

Pawlett House, West Street, Somerton

Somerset TA11 7PS, United Kingdom

www.pushmepress.com

First published in 2013

ISBN: 978-1-909618-06-0

Grateful acknowledgement is made for using "The Road Not Taken" taken from The Poetry of Robert Frost edited by Edward Connery Latham. Published by Jonathan Cape. Reprinted by permission of The Random House Group Ltd.

Grateful acknowledgement is made for using "Do Not Go Gentle Into That Good Night" taken from the Collected Poems of Dylan Thomas. Published by Orion. Reprinted by permission of David Highham Associates Ltd.

Contents

Introduction

The philosopher Nietzsche described his work as 'the greatest gift that (mankind) has ever been given'. The poet Edmund Spenser hoped his book 'The Faery Queen' would transform its readers into noblemen. In comparison, our aims for this book are somewhat more modest.

Designed for pupils as well as for teachers, 'Art of Poetry' is intended to have a number of purposes. A handy exam revision guide as well as a great teaching aid, our book outlines a critical methodology that can be used to tackle the questions on 'unseen' poems which crop up from time to time on examination papers.

Ranging from Elizabethan sonnets to modern free verse, the poems we've chosen are classics which have withstood the test of time and which will withstand the vagaries of examination boards and government agendas. Rather than focusing on poems from one board, such as AQA or OCR, our selection cuts across all the boards. Whatever board you use or study, at GCSE or 'A' level, you will find some of their key poems in 'Art of Poetry'. Hence this book will remain relevant whatever changes examination boards and governments make to the poetry curriculum in schools. We've written the book on poetry we would have liked to have found when we were GCSE pupils wanting to learn how to analyse poems, and then later when we were new to teaching. 'Art of Poetry' should be especially helpful to pupils and to newly qualified teachers, or those simply lacking confidence about the study of poetry. Experienced teachers will, we hope, also find it an interesting and helpful addition to the resources available.

The Structure of the commentaries

Each critical commentary follows broadly the same structure.

Like novels and plays, most poems feature a variety of characters. So the different voices form our first section. We begin by focusing on the narrator, or the voice of the poet. We consider questions such as, who's reciting the poem, what is their relation to the material, are they their own subject as in a lyric poem, are they an objective observer, or do they speak through a character as in a dramatic monologue? For peopleless poems we've stretched our definition to include abstract ideas such as nature, a place or time. Through the lens of character we are able to focus on the central relationships shaping each poem.

What are the key features that distinguish poetry from other literary discourses? Well, poetic language might be one. Poetic language tends to be ordinary language on stilts. In other words, compared to everyday speech the language of poetry is often heightened, and it features a concentration of figurative devices, such as metaphor and symbolism.

These language features are explored under our second heading, imagery. Poetry certainly distinguishes itself from prose through its musical and its formal qualities. In poetry, the rhythm, the tone and the sound of the words are as important as the meanings. We explore how these sonic qualities relate to meanings under the third heading, patterns of sound and sense.

Formal aspects, including metre, rhyme and stanzas, we analyse under the title 'form and structure'. When was the poem written? Who was it written by? How has the poem been interpreted? Such are the sorts of questions related to contexts. For GCSE, contexts of interpretation need only a light touch. We mention contexts in our fifth section only for the light they throw on the poems, and for the potential windows they open for pupils and teachers for further exploration.

In our final sections we summarise the poems in two ways, firstly through 'crunching' them, by which we mean reducing the poem to one word per line. This is a quick but revealing way for readers to engage with prioritising the most significant word in each line of the poem. Following this section are brief summative notes on theme, language, form and context. At the back of the book is a glossary of key technical terms.

We hope teachers and pupils will find these commentaries helpful and illuminating. You probably won't want to read from cover to cover, although this is how it has been designed. We expect that readers will start with the poems they teach or study and then read around them. Deep learning is evident when pupils are able to apply what they have learnt in a new context. Our aspiration is that, as well as providing valuable critical readings on these particular ten poems, this book outlines a clear, systematic model for close reading, one that teachers and pupils can adopt and adapt.

The poems are arranged chronologically. We touch on Renaissance poetry first, move on to The Romantics and then the Victorians, before finishing in the early twentieth century. Somewhere in the mid nineteenth century we also cross the Atlantic to examine some American poems.

NICE TO METRE...

A brief guide to metre and rhythm in poetry

Why express yourself in poetry? Why read words dressed up and expressed as a poem? What can you get from poetry that you can't from prose? There are many compelling answers to these questions. Here though, we're going to concentrate on one aspect of the unique appeal of poetry - the structure of sound in poetry.

Whatever our stage of education, we are all already sophisticated at detecting and using structured sound. Try reading this sentence without any variation whatsoever in how each sound is emphasised, and it will quickly lose what essential human characteristics it had. It will sound robotic. So in a sense, we won't be teaching anything new here. It's just that in poetry the structure of sound is carefully crafted and created. It becomes a key part of what a poem is.

We will introduce a few new key technical terms along the way, but the ideas are straightforward. Individual sounds (syllables) are either stressed (emphasised, sounding louder and longer) or unstressed. As well as clustering into words and sentences for meaning, these sounds (syllables) cluster into rhythmic groups or feet, producing the poem's metre, which is the characteristic way its rhythm works.

In some poems the rhythm is very regular and may even have a name, such as iambic pentameter. At the other extreme a poem may have no discernible regularity at all. This is called free verse. It is vital to remember that the sound in a good poem is structured so that it combines well with the meanings.

For example, take a look at these two lines from Marvell's 'To his Coy Mistress':

'But at my back I alwaies hear

Times winged Chariot hurrying near:'

Forgetting the rhythms for a moment, Marvell is basically saying at this point 'Life is short, Time flies, and it's after us'. Now concentrate on the rhythm of his words.

- In the first line every other syllable is stressed: 'at', 'back', 'al', 'hear'.

- Each syllable before these is unstressed 'But', 'my', 'I', 'aies'.

- This is a regular beat or rhythm which we could write *ti TUM / ti TUM / ti TUM / ti TUM* , with the / separating the feet.

- This type of pattern is called iambic, and because there are four feet in the line, it is tetrameter, so this line is in 'iambic tetrameter'. (Tetra is Greek for four)

- Notice that 'my' and 'I' being unstressed diminishes the speaker, and we are already prepared for what is at his 'back', what he can 'hear' to be bigger than him, since these sounds are stressed.

- On the next line, the iambic rhythm is immediately broken off, since the next line hits us with two consecutive stressed syllables straight off: 'Times' 'wing'. Because a pattern had been established, when it suddenly changes the reader feels it, the words feel crammed together more urgently, the beats of the rhythm are closer, some little parcels of time have gone missing.

A physical rhythmic sensation is created of time slipping away, running out. The sensation is enhanced further by the stress-unstress-unstress pattern of words that follow, 'chariot hurrying' (*TUM-ti-ti, TUM-ti-ti*). So the sounds underscore the meaning of the words.

A few tips and pointers:

- Remember that these sort of effects only happen when a poem runs through a human brain and out loud to a human ear.

- Try not to think of a poem as an object, out there, in the world. It's a composed field of language, more like a piece of software.

- Remember that the marks you see on the page are not themselves the poem, they are the notation for it, like a score is for a piece of music.

- Always read the poems aloud, try to get a feel for their physical effects. Readers need to be open to them, to have their brains in 'compatibility mode', after all some of them were designed to run on 'English 1598'.

- By running them through your mind you are getting direct access to the world from which they came.

and yet by hea
I think my love a.
As any she beli
with false compar

Sonnet 130 - My Mistress' Eyes Are Nothing Like the Sun

My mistress' eyes are nothing like the sun;
Coral is far more red than her lips' red;
If snow be white, why then her breasts are dun;
If hairs be wires, black wires grow on her head.
I have seen roses damask'd, red and white,
But no such roses see I in her cheeks;
And in some perfumes is there more delight
Than in the breath that from my mistress reeks.
I love to hear her speak, yet well I know
That music hath a far more pleasing sound;
I grant I never saw a goddess go;
My mistress, when she walks, treads on the ground:
And yet, by heaven, I think my love as rare
As any she belied with false compare.

William Shakespeare (1609)

CHARACTERS

Narrator

The use of the first person pronoun 'I' is an indication that this poem will present the poet's own feelings about the nature of real love. This sonnet contains humorous mockery of the overblown metaphors used by some 'sonneteers' (writers of sonnets) and although the description of the narrator's lady love is frank, the honesty of the narrator leaves the reader feeling that this is a genuine relationship.

Shakespeare is mischievously presenting an alternative to typical **RENAISSANCE** love poetry, where women are often compared to nature, but then shown to outstrip it, (sun, coral, snow, roses, perfume, music, goddesses). This is where the 'goddess' idea comes from in more conventional sonnets.

The narrator's purpose is made clear in the final line: He is warning about the perils of empty praise – 'false compare'.

There is a playfulness about the sonnet which is highly entertaining and accessible. The comparisons the narrator makes about his mistress are very recognisably romantic and it is the fact that he then says she's not like any of these which makes the sonnet comical.

Mistress

The mistress is presented through the senses of the narrator.

We end up with a character like a real person because of the honest way she is described. The mistress is not named but the use of 'my' might be seen as a specific enough reference. After all, she is the narrator's mistress so perhaps it wouldn't be tactful to reveal her name. In any case the lack of a name makes the poem more universal and certainly doesn't diminish the sense of her robust reality.

The mistress is initially presented very physically:

1. She is black haired, with a dark skin-tone (dun).

2. Her lips are 'red', but not too red.

3. Her eyes are 'nothing like the sun', which might indicate dark eyes.

4. Her movement is revealed; she 'treads on the ground' when she walks which suggests perhaps heavy-footedness, but could also show that the narrator appreciates her for her down-to-earth qualities.

5. Her breasts also feature in the inventory.

This list of physical attributes is presented in a manner that might be seen as dismissive, sexist even. Indeed, the verb 'reeks' is used to describe her breath moving us from the sense of sight to the sense of smell, a sense not often used in love poetry.

It's worth considering that the narrator dwells on the physical.

Her intellectual or spiritual qualities are never referred to.

The description of the woman is interesting in the context of the time the poem was written (1590s) because the Elizabethan ideal of beauty was very fair. This woman's darkness is exotic and we get a strong sense of a real person despite (or because of) Shakespeare's depiction.

It is reminiscent of Jessie J rather than Mia Wasikowska, or Monica Bellucci rather than Nicole Kidman.

'Roses, damasked red and white' alludes to the Tudor rose: the red and white rose was the **EMBLEM** of the Tudor dynasty of which Elizabeth I was the last. If you look at paintings of Elizabeth I, you can see why the pale and interesting look was so fashionable. The Virgin Queen's almost supernatural aura explains why **HYPERBOLIC** hymns of praise to female beauty became so popular with aristocratic sonnet writers during her reign.

IMAGERY

The main object in the poem is the mistress. She is then compared with a variety of things that are ultimately found to be inadequate or unrealistic: the sun, coral, snow, roses, perfume, music and goddesses.

The imagery in this poem is sparse and the effects could really be described as anti-imagery. The poet dismisses all the usual ways of trying to elevate a woman's beauty in poetical terms.

Shakespeare chooses clichéd ideas and then proceeds to demolish them, by showing how utterly silly they are in terms of describing a real, flesh and blood lover.

He has the skill to take the devices of lesser poets, knock them flat and **PARODY** them (something which mimics and mocks) and still deliver a vigorously appreciative appraisal of his mistress.

In the first quatrain the subject matter is given a brutally honest treatment as Shakespeare takes the tired old similes of the Elizabethan love sonnet and compares them to a real woman:

1. Her eyes are 'nothing like the sun.'

2. Her lips are not as red as coral.

3. Her breasts are light brown, not white.

If her hair is described as a series of 'wires', a common image among poets of the time, then hers are black.

Despite all the seeming denial, Shakespeare actually conveys genuine regard for the woman's physical attributes; her eyes, lips, breasts (and cheeks) are all catalogued and this is what Shakespeare manages to emphasise, without the need of far-fetched comparisons.

Repetition is used to highlight the futility of comparing things which turn out to be fundamentally different; 'red' is applied to coral, lips and roses:

1. 'Roses' is used both literally and figuratively (the supposed 'roses' in a woman's cheeks).

2. 'Black' is applied to 'wires' and hair.

The repetition also, perhaps, conveys a tone of disbelief at how such absurd exaggeration could ever be sincere.

It's also clear that much of the focus on colour is quite extreme; red, white and black are strong, emblematic colours.

The woman in question does have red lips and black hair, suggesting passion, danger and vitality. The fact that her breasts are not white might similarly suggest that she is not insipid and conventional but passionate and vivacious.

The concept that usually provokes the biggest reaction from the modern reader is the assertion that his mistress' breath 'reeks'. It is a striking assertion, but contextually it is not surprising. In Elizabethan times perfumes were distilled from all sorts of unpleasant things to make very strong smelling products. They had to be strong smelling because most people stank in a way modern readers can't begin to imagine.

To have 'reeky' breath might be unpleasant, but it wouldn't be unusual and in this poem it adds to the forceful realism of the portrayal. Besides, the word 'reeks' wasn't as strong to Elizabethans as it is to us, so perhaps we can excuse the seeming bluntness of the narrator.

Far-fetched comparisons typically listed a woman's assets comparing them to other lovely, natural things.

This is why the narrator acknowledges the potential points of comparison (sun, coral, snow, roses, perfume, music, goddesses) but then mocks the genre by dismissing them.

It is the dismissal of conventional comparisons and the use of negatives which creates the sense of an argument throughout the poem.

However, it is the final rhyming couplet where the clout of the sonnet comes.

After twelve lines of scepticism, the poet appeals to heaven, describes his lover as 'rare' (precious/unusual). He also delivers his highest praise, that all other women immortalised in poetry were 'belied with false compare' that is, described using hopelessly exaggerated language. They were, in effect, being lied about.

The final couplet offers the answer to the questions the poet has posed throughout the preceding twelve lines and works like a punchline.

PATTERNS OF SOUND AND SENSE

Look at the repeated phrases on which the comparison is constructed. As much as the images themselves, these **COMPARATIVE DISCOURSE MARKERS** signal Shakespeare's disdain for the wildly exaggerated and therefore false comparisons used by conventional sonneteers.

- 'nothing like'

- 'far more' (used in 2 lines and 10)

- 'why then'

- 'no such'

- 'I never saw'

With the exclamatory phrase 'by heaven!', these seemingly unimportant phrases also contribute significantly to the sense of the narrator's speaking voice and his character.

FORM AND STRUCTURE

The poem takes the form of a Shakespearean sonnet.

The word sonnet is derived from the Italian for 'little song' and was usually used to express and explore the nature of love in the Elizabethan period. Here Shakespeare isn't just writing a love sonnet to someone though, he's actually subverting the whole genre of sonnet writing. Cross rhymed lines (abab, cdcd,efef) give a sense of progression which is brought to a conclusion by means of the thought provoking rhyming couplet at the end (gg), which works like a punchline. The sudden change of mood from the previous quatrain to the final couplet, called the **VOLTA,** signifies a change of mood or alternative point of view.

Metre

Scan the lines and you will find that the metre used is iambic pentameter i.e five - beat lines going Ti-TUM.

However, in line two the first foot (unit of rhythm) isn't iambic. It goes TUM-Ti which just alters the rhythm enough to make us sit up and take notice. This type of foot is called a **TROCHEE**. The stress falls on the first syllable of '**CO**ral' and this signals a shift as the narrator begins to consider other things that his lover is not like.

The choice of iambic pentameter is integral to the form of a sonnet, but it's worth remembering that iambic pentameter is often the form of serious poetry.

It's also the poetical metre which best mimics the patterns of speech in English whilst the iamb is mimetic of the heartbeat.

All of which influences the way we might read and understand this poem as a critique of false affections and genuine love.

Stanza and rhyme scheme

Shakespeare's sonnets don't have stanzas (separate groups of lines, like paragraphs in prose) but the groups of four lines, or quatrains, contribute a similar sense of development that different stanzas might.

- The first quatrain describes the mistress' appearance in frank terms.

- The second is more fanciful and moves away from the woman to use another point of comparison – roses, the sight of which links to the idea of perfume (smell) enabling Shakespeare to deliver the killer line on reeking breath. These two quatrains form the **OCTAVE** (the first 8 lines of a sonnet) which is primarily concerned with what the woman is not like.

- The third quatrain focuses on the sound and motion of his mistress and, with the final couplet, forms the last six lines, known as the **SESTET** of the sonnet. Here the poem shifts away from the negative comparison of the octave to more objective description; he 'loves to hear her speak' and she 'walks...on the ground'.

The final couplet gives an example of a **VOLTA**. This often comes in line nine of a sonnet. Here the sudden move towards praise is very near the end. This contributes to the impact of the sincerity of what the poet expresses in the couplet, making the reader reconsider the 'criticisms' of earlier in the poem. The volta forces us to ask whether it was the woman or other poets who were in the firing line. If we thought the poet was harsh on his lover, we can see with greater clarity Shakespeare's mockery of other poets.

The rhyme scheme is **MASCULINE**, which means the rhymes land on the stressed second beat of the **IAMB**. If we crunch the poem to focus only on the rhyming words we get:

- **Sun - Red - Dun - Head**
- **White - Cheeks - Delight - Reeks**
- **Know - Sound - Go - Ground**
- **Rare - Compare**

The fully masculine rhyme scheme is wholly appropriate because this poem is written from a masculine perspective. It offers a **male gaze** (a point of view that is particularly male and which treats women as objects) and so feminine rhymes (when the rhyme falls on an unstressed beat as in Sonnet 116) would be less appropriate.

Enjambment and caesurae

The poem is heavily reliant on enjambment. Shakespeare is very adept at exploiting the possibilities of iambic pentameter without being restricted by the form.

The combination of enjambment and caesurae are the means by which he flexes the form of the poem.

In these first four lines, each comparison has its own line, which contributes hugely to the sense of denial. There is no room for manoeuvre; the narrator thinks such florid ideas are nonsense.

By the second quatrain, the narrator allows himself to consider roses and because the idea is more elaborate and because he is introducing wider knowledge, **the lines need to run on to accommodate the elasticity of the idea**. There is a check at the end of line 6. But the perfume of roses is suggested in the next line which then runs on to conclude so devastatingly with 'reeks'.

Music and movement are the focus of the third quatrain. Each concept has its own run-on line, but there isn't enjambment between the two. Neatly this keeps each idea separate.

CONTEXT

Shakespeare wrote 154 sonnets, first published in the 1609 quarto. They take the form of sequences, some of which seem to be addressed to a 'fair' young man and some being to a 'dark lady' as in this sonnet. To add to the mystery, Shakespeare also dedicated the publication to a 'Mr WH' whose identity has never been confirmed. Sonnets were something of a craze. Many poets were inspired by the Italian writer Petrarch, who had fashioned sonnets (little songs) to his idealised love, Laura.

By Shakespeare's time, many of the conventions of sonnet writing had already become tired. His sonnet takes these Petrarchan conventions and plays about with them in such a way that Shakespeare manages to reveal how silly they had become, whilst at the same time showing that he could do it better. And we are left with a more honest declaration of love despite all the attempts to demolish the foolishness of the form.

The listing of desirable female qualities isn't only found in the sonnets. Shakespeare also uses the device in his plays. In 'Twelfth Night' Olivia pours scorn on Count Orsino's declarations of love by listing his requirements in a woman, which reveals that the Count's isn't real love, just idealised love. Similarly in 'Much Ado About Nothing' both Beatrice and Benedick use lists as a way of revealing their ideal partners, which in turn show us that they have yet to acknowledge real love.

THE POEM CRUNCHED

Try to reduce the poem to just one word for each line. Here's one version:

Mistress – red – breasts – wires – roses – cheeks – perfumes – reeks – speak – music – goddess – ground – rare – false

KEY REVISION

Themes

- Accurate description of a lover.

- The nature of female beauty.

- Mocks the empty praise and insincerity of clichéd poems

- Real, true, sincere love shown through contrast

Language

- Uses conventions of clichéd Elizabethan love poetry to undermine and mock them.

- Comparisons are with natural elements.

Form and Structure

- Elizabethan/Shakespearean sonnet.

- The volta comes late for added impact.

- Not much in the way of enjambment which reflects terse dismissal of outlandish love poetry.

True or False? Shakespeare's poems were in fact written by Marlowe.

Just so much honor, when thou yield'st to me,
Will waste, as this flea's death took life from thee

The Flea

Mark but this flea, and mark in this,
How little that which thou deniest me is;
It sucked me first, and now sucks thee,
And in this flea our two bloods mingled be;
Thou know'st that this cannot be said
A sin, nor shame, nor loss of maidenhead,
Yet this enjoys before it woo,
And pampered swells with one blood made of two,
And this, alas, is more than we would do.

Oh stay, three lives in one flea spare,
Where we almost, nay more than married are.
This flea is you and I, and this
Our mariage bed, and marriage temple is;
Though parents grudge, and you, w'are met,
And cloistered in these living walls of jet.
Though use make you apt to kill me,
Let not to that, self-murder added be,
And sacrilege, three sins in killing three.

Cruel and sudden, hast thou since
Purpled thy nail, in blood of innocence?

Wherein could this flea guilty be,

Except in that drop which it sucked from thee?

Yet thou triumph'st, and say'st that thou

Find'st not thy self, nor me the weaker now;

'Tis true; then learn how false, fears be:

Just so much honour, when thou yield'st to me,

Will waste, as this flea's death took life from thee.

John Donne (circa 1630)

CHARACTERS

Narrator

Initially the narrator's voice is a masterful one. From the outset Donne adopts a commanding tone, as in the first **IMPERATIVE** active verb, 'mark but this flea, and mark in this...' and in the second 'confess...'.

Like a teacher, lawyer or priest, the poet is instructing his audience, talking down to them from a position of authority.

The opening double imperative ('mark' and 'mark') is underscored by insistent monosyllables, and the 'but' makes it sound as if this argument is going to be pretty straightforward and convincing. Clearly this is a man setting about the task of seduction with some relish.

However, the tone changes dramatically in the second stanza. Shocked by her actions, the narrator pleads with his lady not to kill the flea. The exclamatory 'oh stay...(your hand)' signals that power is shifting from the narrator to his beloved. The assured masculine voice sounds suddenly squeaky and unconvincing, 'Cruel and sudden...'. This accusatory tone is, perhaps, stereotypically feminine.

But the poem concludes with the narrator very much back in charge. Recovering his manliness, he emphasises the lesson to be learnt: 'Then learn how false, fears be'. Once again he is the imparter of knowledge, like a teacher, sermoniser or lawyer.

It's important to remember though that Donne is not really trying to make his argument persuasive. This is a comical poem and the poet is not being entirely serious.

His tongue is firmly in his cheek.

Effectively 'The Flea' is a courtship ritual, like the elaborate dances performed by male birds to attract a mate. What makes Donne attractive?

- In this ritual of seduction Donne's plumage is his daring and his wit.

- His rejection of dull conventions shows his boldness.

- His sexual language shows his daring sauciness.

- His ability to play around with words to bend argument to his will demonstrates his cleverness.

- His self-mockery shows his self-awareness.

To successfully seduce his lady Donne needs to argue very skilfully. Fortunately, he was exceptionally well trained in rhetoric, having studied to be a lawyer. He must persuade his lady to reject anything that stands in the way of his lust: social conventions, morality, honour, their parents wishes, her modesty must all be vanquished and swept aside by the tide of his language. Presumably she also needs to find him attractive too.

The argument centres on the **EXTENDED METAPHOR** (or what is technically called a **CONCEIT**) of the flea. Strip it of its elaborate style the argument does not seem entirely convincing:

- First the poet points out that the flea has bitten both of them.

- Therefore, he says, their blood has been 'mingled' inside the flea.

- Which means they have had sexual intercourse, in a way, yet the woman has not lost her virginity ('maidenhead'). (Note: 'Bloods mingled be' is a euphemism for sex).

And how sad it is, bemoans the poet (look at that heart sore and melodramatic 'alas') that the flea has the pleasures denied to the poet and his lady. When the lady expresses her feelings about this argument in the second stanza the poet has to take up a new tack.

- Inside the flea, he explains, all three are married.

- Therefore the inside of the flea is a 'marriage temple',

- So, if she killed the flea, not only will she commit 'self-murder', and kill Donne and the flea, which would be sins in themselves, she will also commit another sin of sacrilege by destroying the 'marriage temple'.

Who wouldn't be bowled over by this masterful argument? Not this woman, evidently.

Unimpressed by his feeble wit, she kills the flea in the last stanza.

And with that decisively destructive act it seems Donne has lost the argument and failed in his seduction. The lady appears to have the upper hand, as the poet acknowledges, 'thou triumph'st'.

Now the poet has just three lines to turn the situation on its head, to snatch victory from the jaws of defeat. This would seem an impossible task. He manages it by saying that as the fear of the result of killing the flea has proved unfounded, as it has not led to the deaths of the lovers, so she should see '**HOW FALSE, FEARS BE**'. Therefore she need not fear losing her honour.

Is she convinced? Perhaps she will give the poet high marks for trying.

What overall impression do we form of the poet in his guise as narrator? He makes a witty and daring argument. He can be masterful and clever. He is eloquent and persuasive. He can present himself in a comic light. Perhaps too he is a little arrogant and rather lustful.

Think of the poem as a very elaborate "chat-up" conversation.

Whatever you think of Donne's attitude to women, you might agree that he has gone to great lengths to produce something more original and witty than the usual clichéd chat up lines, such as 'I hope you have a library card because I'm checking you out.'

The poet's daring rejection of strict religious and social conventions and the authority of parents, his desire to get on and 'live life to the full' also make him seem rather modern and, I think, persuasive.

His beloved

Addressed throughout the poem, the lady is given no words. To some critics this shows Donne's treatment of the woman as an object of lust.

However the beloved is far from passive. At the start of the poem she has the power to deny Donne his sexual desires. She listens, presumably patiently, to his frankly far-fetched argument that they have 'kind of already had sex because they've both been bitten by the flea'. Her feelings are expressed at the start of the second stanza when the poet has to beg her not to squash the flea.

'Oh stay, three lives in one flea spare...'

The lady is even less impressed by the absurd argument the increasingly desperate poet puts forward in the second stanza. Who's the fool here, if not the poet?

Her response this time is swift and emphatic; she squashes the flea with her nail, much to the poet's horror and alarm:

'Cruel and sudden, hast thou since/ purpled thy nail, in blood of *innocence?'*

She has the power to destroy his argument and to destroy his symbol of their love, just with her fingertip. That is all the weaponry she needs. As the war imagery signals, she is certainly not just a passive victim, she is the victor: 'thou triumph'st'. But in the final triplet of the poem the tables are turned again and Donne is arguably back in charge. Whether he had won the argument we'll never know, but he gives himself the last say, naturally.

Though she is silent, the impression of this lady is of someone formidable, someone who can see straight through Donne's sophistry (false arguments) and act decisively (squashing the flea). But she is also someone who might be seduced by such entertaining and extravagant, self-mocking wit.

The flea

Donne uses the flea as a symbol of love and marriage.

Stop and think about that for a moment. Donne uses a **FLEA** as a symbol of **LOVE**. This is a strikingly unlikely comparison. Fleas are disgusting, repulsive parasites, irritants and disease carriers. How can a flea be a 'marriage temple'? The idea is clearly preposterous.

And that's the point. For Renaissance writers, such as Donne or Shakespeare, the quality of one's wit was tested and demonstrated by the ability to make two things wholly unlike appear to be the same.

Donne knows that it's a ridiculous argument. His beloved knows it's a ridiculous argument. The reader knows it too. The challenge for Donne is to make it sound at all convincing; the entertainment is in seeing him struggling with the task.

The flea is described as being like a 'bed', as being 'pampered', as 'swelling', as a 'marriage temple' and as having royal blood 'purpled'. Because of, or despite all this, it is killed. Thus the dynamics of power between the couple are revealed through the descriptions and treatment of the flea. The extended comparison of the flea is called a **CONCEIT**.

IMAGERY

What key objects do we have in the poem?

Clearly we have the flea. As we have seen, this is metaphorised into a bed and a temple and so forth. We also have some sexual, religious, colour and battle imagery.

Donne's suggestive sexual imagery includes the repeated use of the verb 'suck', as well as 'bloods mingled' and 'pampered swells'.

It is part of Donne's outrageously bold attitude that he is prepared to use such taboo sexual language in his love poem. It's still somewhat shocking now, even in the twenty-first century. Think how shocking this must have been in the 1600s. (It's important here to remember that Donne did not intend these early poems to be published; rather they were circulated privately around a small group of male friends.)

Whether this sexual language is erotically seductive, or not, we'll leave to you, the reader, to decide.

Donne employs religious imagery in an equally controversial way.

To use religion as a tool of seduction, to play so fast and loose with the serious concept of sin, could be seen as another example of Donne's audacity, or be seen simply as blasphemous. Later in life, when he had become the highly respectable establishment Dean of St Paul's Cathedral, he may have regretted this saucy irreverence.

- The poet describes the lovers as 'married' in the flea.

- Inside its body, which is a 'marriage temple' is their 'marriage bed'.

- Continuing the metaphor he says that they are 'cloistered' within the flea.

Remember that marriage is a holy sacrament and you'll see how bold (or disrespectful) Donne is being. The use of the colour 'purple' could also be seen to be impudent, as this was the colour of religious authority as well as of royalty.

By describing the flea's blood as purple Donne raises the lovers to the level of monarchs, so cleverly flattering his beloved.

Battle imagery reveals the dynamics of power. After the killing of the flea the lady 'triumphs't'. But when Donne turns the tables in the final triplet it is she who 'yield'st'. Notice too the confident use of the word '**WHEN**'; 'when thou yield'st', not '**IF** thou…'

The language conveys a mood of confidence that he will prevail.

PATTERNS OF SOUND AND SENSE

Repetition is a key poetic device for all poets. Donne uses repetition of significant words, such as 'sucks', 'marriage' and 'sins', as well as phrases, such as 'mark…this'.

He also uses the sounds of words to create effects. Look, for example, at the sensuous sibilance in the line 'sucked first, and now sucks thee'. But the major patterning technique he uses in this poem is the rhetorical tool of antithesis.

ANTITHESIS was a key device for Renaissance writers. It is the use of balanced opposites. It can work on a scale starting with a phrase, working up to a stanza, and then develop across a whole text.

In the first stanza the flea and the male lover are presented as an antithetical pair.

The flea has tasted the flesh of the beloved, unlike Donne. Moreover the flea has taken its pleasure without having to go through the elaborate (and time consuming) process of courtship of which the poem is part, unlike Donne: '…this enjoys before it woo'.

In the third the cruelty of the woman contrasts with the 'innocence' of the flea, a word that is also picked up with its opposite, 'guilty'. The woman's triumph is the opposite to her yielding to Donne. And as the antitheses build up, that which is 'true' is contrasted with what is 'false'.

Donne's use of antithesis is a major characteristic of his poetry. Another related device is his use of paradox or apparent contradiction. For Donne the central paradox in life is that we have to die to reach eternal life.

In 'The Flea' he tries to argue something paradoxical – that the woman is still a virgin despite having sexual intercourse and that though they have not had a wedding the lovers are married already. This paradoxical style is typical of Donne.

FORM AND STRUCTURE

The poem is exceptionally elegantly constructed, built upon patterns of twos and threes.

Metre

Conventionally Renaissance poems were written in single dominant metre, such as iambic pentameter. It is characteristic of Donne that he flouts this artistic convention, just as he flouts conventions about sex and religion.

His metrical pattern is more irregular and has a rougher, less silky texture than usually thought desirable. Donne wanted his verse to have the quality of impassioned speech.

A few examples show the pattern and how he deviates from it.

In the first stanza the poet starts with an arguably strong stress on 'mark' and follows it with another strong stress on 'but'. Then 'flea', 'mark' and 'this' are also stressed. So the first line is:

> *'Mark but this flea, and mark in this'*
> *TUM, TUM, ti-TUM, ti-TUM, ti-TUM*

The irregular pattern of the first foot gives way to a regular iambic pattern.

The second line is more regular, with only the fourth beat switched, to lend emphasis to 'deny'st':

> *'How little that which thou deny'st me is'*
> *Ti-TUM, ti-TUM, ti-TUM, TUM-ti, ti-TUM*

The third line is more irregular, and hard to scan:

'Me it sucked first, and now sucks thee'
TUM-Ti, TUM-ti, ti-TUM, ti-TUM

Or perhaps,

TUM–Ti, TUM TUM, ti, TUM TUM TUM

Stanzas & Rhyme Scheme

If the metre plays fast and loose with an iambic pattern, the form of the stanzas and the rhyme scheme provide a counterbalancing regularity, elegance and poise. In particular Donne plays around with the idea of twos (the 2 lovers) and threes (the lovers plus the flea).

The poem's form is like an elaborate dance of twos and threes.

There are three even, regular stanzas. Each of these is composed of three couplets (two consecutive lines rhyming with each other) and each ends with a triple rhyme, or **TRIPLET**. It is also noticeable that all the rhymes are full masculine ones, helping re-enforce the sense of male vigour.

Enjambment and caesurae

Enjambment connects lines and stanzas; caesurae break lines up. They often work in tandem. In Donne's hands the caesurae create the patterns and rhythms of a spoken voice, one that is carefully weighing and balancing each thought to find the exactly right expression.

Look, for instance, at the number of lines split by commas. The general effect is one of unhurried reflective and measured thought. In lines such

as 'when we almost, nay more than married are' the caesura creates the
sense of the poet modifying his line as he alters his thoughts. Thus the
poem feels immediate and dramatic.

CONTEXTS

Biographical Context

A childhood prodigy who studied at Oxford when just eleven years old,
as a young man Donne had a reputation for being something of 'a ladies'
man'. As a contemporary commented, 'he was a frequent visitor of the
ladies'. Training to be a young lawyer in London it appears he lived an
extravagant and rather dubious lifestyle.

**The sexually charged, daring tone of 'The Flea' and its cavalier
attitude to conventional sexual morality fits well with this picture
of the young Donne.**

Having reformed himself, later in life he became the Dean of St Paul's,
one of the highest positions in the Church of England. It is highly
significant that Donne was born Catholic, but converted as a young man
to Protestantism. He lived in a time when to be a Catholic in England
was to be at a significant disadvantage as Catholics were banned from
all the professions and viewed with suspicion as potential traitors by the
crown.

**There is a boldness in Donne's actions, or perhaps a shrewd eye
for the main chance.**

THE POEM CRUNCHED

Before reading our list, have a go at crunching the poem. This means reducing each line to just one word. Think carefully about which word you think is the most important one in each line, write this down and then compare.

Mark - deny'st – sucks – mingled – confess – sin – enjoys – pampered – alas – stay – married – flea – bed – parents – cloistered - kill – murder – sacrilege – cruel – innocence – guilty – drop - triumph'st – weaker – learn - yield'st - life

KEY REVISION

Themes

- A form of love poem, aimed at seducing the woman through a demonstration of wit.

- Courtship as a kind of conquest.

- Expresses a carpe diem message, let's get on with it - 'seize the day' in Latin.

Language

- Like other Metaphysical poets Donne builds the poem around an extended metaphor, or **CONCEIT**. Compares the flea to a lover, to a bed, to a temple.

- Many rhetorical tricks to persuade his beloved, **ANTITHESIS**, commands, rhetorical questions, and patterns of three: 'a sin, or shame, or loss of maidenhead'.

- Complex language, like the elevated speech of a lawyer - its wit, balance and poise expressing the poet's character.

- Humour is created through the use of elevated language applied to the 'low' subject of seduction.

Form and structure

- The form is like a complex and elegant dance.

- Donne plays around with patterns of twos and threes, encoding the relationship between him, his beloved and the flea into the structure of the poem.

Contexts

- Donne is a Renaissance writer; his demonstration of wit through finding similarities between things wholly different is a typical demonstration of Renaissance wit.

- He was part of a group of writers labelled the Metaphysicals, famous for daring and shocking use of imagery, and for the pioneering of the extended metaphor.

True of false? When Donne was arrested for secretly marrying the young niece of his employer he expressed his unfortunate situation with the comment, 'John Donne Anne Donne, undone'.

Marks of weakness
marks of woe

London

I wander thro' each charter'd street,
Near where the charter'd Thames does flow,
And mark in every face I meet
Marks of weakness, marks of woe.

In every cry of every Man,
In every Infant's cry of fear,
In every voice, in every ban,
The mind-forg'd manacles I hear.

How the Chimney-sweeper's cry
Every black'ning Church appalls;
And the hapless Soldier's sigh
Runs in blood down Palace walls.

But most thro' midnight streets I hear
How the youthful Harlot's curse
Blasts the new born Infant's tear,
And blights with plagues the Marriage hearse.

William Blake - published in 1794

CHARACTERS

Narrator

The use of the first person pronoun 'I' indicates that this is a **LYRIC** poem expressing the poet's own feelings, or those of his persona, about England's capital city. The verbs associated with the narrator are:

- 'I wander'

- 'Mark'

- 'I meet'

- 'I hear'.

'Wander' emphasizes the idea that exploitation in London is universal; Blake doesn't have to search for it; it's everywhere. Whatever direction he takes he'll find it. Though they are in the active voice, the verbs suggest that the poet is fairly passive – he's a witness, registering his impressions, rather than a participant in the world of the poem.

Look at the line: 'and mark in every face I meet/ marks of weakness, marks of woe'. 'Mark' is used here first as a verb and then as a noun, and a word shared by narrator and characters. Blake could easily have chosen a different verb, such as 'see' or 'notice'. As well as a poet, Blake was a visual artist. He engraved the pictures that accompanied the poems in '**SONGS OF INNOCENCE AND EXPERIENCE**', which means he would have had to cut into metal. The emphatic strength of the verb 'mark' conveys permanence. 'Mark' also implies something doomed, as in the mark of Cain (Genesis 4:12), or, in Harry Potter, the 'dark mark'.

Crowd

What are these rough sorts of people doing traipsing through the enchanted garden of English poetry?

The crowd represents the ordinary masses, the common people, whose suffering is so often ignored by those in power. The repetition of the **ADJECTIVE** 'every' emphasizes Blake's idea that every human being matters and that the suffering is universal. Over in France, Europe's leaders had witnessed the first successful rebellion of the commoners in history. The British government responded with a harsh crack down on freedom.

Blake's poem protests against the destructive effect of the powerful on the powerless.

The soldier, the sweep and the prostitute

The individual characters are symbols or emblems of exploitation. The sweep would have been a young boy sold into a very harsh form of slavery (see Blake's two Chimney Sweeper poems in 'Songs of Innocence and Experience'). Abused and brutalised, sweeps were seen as the lowest form of human life.

The soldier's body and blood is used to protect the state and the monarchy. So Blake boldly signals that the King has blood on his hands.

The prostitute is the worst example of exploitation for Blake because he believed love was sacred. The poet was appalled by sex and love being commodified, bought and sold like any other goods.

This sexual exploitation causes the destruction of innocence and new life, embodied by the child who is 'blasted' by disease (the 'Harlot's curse').

Disease also spreads into society, carried from prostitute to client, and into marriage. The result is premature death ('hearse').

IMAGERY

What objects do we have in the poem? The chartered streets and Thames; the manacles; the blackening church, the palace and the hearse.

This is a poem full of **AURAL** as well as **VISUAL IMAGERY**: the voices of the Londoners, the clink of their mental manacles, the cries of the sweepers, the cursing of the prostitute. For Romantic Poets Nature was sacred. Nature was the manifestation of God on earth and a great source of poetic inspiration.

This unhappy, discordant and diseased city seems the exact opposite of the sacred beauty of Nature.

The land and the water are both 'chartered' – they have been mapped, come under commercial control, become property to be bought and sold by chartered companies. However the verb 'flows', with its slight echo of 'wander', suggests that the water has the potential to escape this control. For Blake the Church was part of the corrupt, oppressive state.

The churches are 'black'ning' because they should be an active voice of protest against the exploitation of children. The failure of the church blackens its name and its bricks.

The image of the soldier's 'sigh' running in 'blood down palace walls' is extraordinary in two ways: firstly Blake transforms the sound 'sigh' into something visual. This mixing of senses is called a **SYNAESTHETIC EFFECT** and has a nightmarish, disorientating quality. Secondly Blake is incredibly bold in pointing the finger of blame at the monarchy.

Rather than the blood being on the King's hands, it is running down his walls.

This was a very dangerous thing to say in England in 1792. This was a time when some of Blake's fellow political radicals were being arrested by the government and attacked by pro monarchy gangs. Such comments could be seen as treasonous. And the penalty for treason could be death.

The image of the 'mind forg'd manacles' is one of Blake's most celebrated. It is characteristic of Blake because it combines something abstract with something concrete – 'mind' is abstract; 'manacles' concrete.

This is a very potent way to help us to imagine or visualise an idea.

The idea of mental chains, people's thoughts being locked, imprisoned and controlled; in other words the 'mind forg'd manacles' is an image of brainwashing.

Blake does not make it clear who makes these manacles. It could be that they are made by the state, through propaganda. But they could also be self-inflicted, formed by blinkered perceptions and ways of seeing the world. In either case, arguably there is hope - these aren't real chains; they are 'mind forg'd' and perceptions can be changed, by art or by poetry.

The verb 'forg'd' is doubly appropriate. It is an image drawn from metal work, but it is also a pun. These perceptions of reality are forgeries, false ideas that can and must be replaced by the truth.

Arguably the most powerful image of the poem is the last one. Note how the structure of the poem narrows from the landscape, to the crowds, to the single emblematic figures. Like a film camera we pan the scene and then zoom in, as day changes to night, to finish at moral midnight and the 'youthful harlot'.

Blake's image of sexual infection is a metaphor for moral corruption.

The disease spreads through time and space; it will be passed down the generations, from the prostitute to children. Carried from prostitute to client, it will infect marriage. The destruction this process will wreak is conveyed by:

- Violent **PLOSIVE** and alliterative verbs, 'blasts', the biblical 'blights'.

- Through the similarly biblical resonance of 'plagues', where Blake evokes the idea of God's punishment of sin.

- The **OXYMORON** 'marriage hearse' shows that this corruption is so potent it can even transform a celebration of new life into a shocking image of death. It's like something out of 'Night of the Living Dead'.

PATTERNS OF SOUND AND SENSE

Repetition is a key poetic device for all poets, but it is especially important for Blake. It falls into different categories: **DICTION; SYNTAX**; images; sounds.

- Look at all the 'ins', 'ands', 'everys'; the 'chartered', 'mark', and 'cries'.

- As well as repetition of single words there is repetition of syntax: 'in every...in every...in every' and of phrases, such as 'I hear'.

- You will have noticed too the alliterative sound patterns of 'Marks of Weakness, Marks of Woe', 'mind-forg'd manacles', 'most through midnight', and the **PLOSIVE**, 'blasts' and 'blights'.

The images are further examples of repetition: the chimney sweep, the soldier and the prostitute are three versions of the same figure: the individual exploited by those with power.

What is the effect of the repetition?

As well as building and increasing rhetorical emphasis the repetition creates a powerful rhythmical charge, reminiscent of spells, chants or incantations.

The insistent repetition also creates an almost claustrophobic sound world, one that is, perhaps, an aural equivalent of the oppression Blake is describing. Emotion that is only just under control has explosive potential. The restrictions in sounds and vocabulary just about keep Blake's emotions in check.

The rhyme scheme is cross-rhyme in **QUATRAINS**: ABAB, CDCD, and so forth. All the rhymes are **MASCULINE**, where the line ends with a stress. This rhyme choice makes a further contribution to the concentrated intensity of the poem. For example, in the fourth line the stress starts with a strong stress on 'marks' and ends with another strong stress on 'woe'. Try swapping the line around to 'marks of woe, marks of weakness' and you'll see that this would create a weak stress at the end. If 'weakness' rhymes with another end word this makes an example of what's called **FEMININE** rhyme. Hopefully you can see how Blake's version concentrates stresses and so sounds stronger, more intense, more emphatic.

FORM AND STRUCTURE

Metre

Scan the first stanza and you'll find that the first, second and third lines are written in clear iambic tetrameter, i.e. four beat lines going Ti-TUM, ti-TUM, ti-TUM, ti-TUM. The fourth line switches, however, to **TROCHAIC TETRAMETER**: TUM-ti, TUM-ti, TUM-ti, TUM...

Some lines in the rest of the poem follow the iambic pattern:

'In **eve**ry **cry** of **eve**ry **man**'
Ti-Tum, ti-Tum, ti-Tum, ti-TUM

While others reverse the pattern:
'How the **chimn**ey-**sweep**er's **cry'**
TUM-ti, TUM-ti, TUM-ti, TUM

So we have the idea of reversal, or inversion, encoded in the metre, and in the trochaic lines a movement in stress from strong at the start to strong at the end of the line.

Traditionally, in well-made poems it was expected that the poet keep to one dominant metre. **FLEXING THE METRE** in this way shows Blake's disregard for rules and his desire to create poems that are more raw, more real and roughly textured. It suggests the emotional content of the poem is so strong it breaks through the formal constraints. Like rap music today, Blake's poetry was 'real' - the literature of the street.

Tetrameter also helps to make poetry accessible to people. In comparison to pentameter, which is often the metre of serious verse in English, the four beat tetrameter is a more common metre widely used in songs.

Stanzas

We have 4 stanzas of 4 lines (quatrains) with 4 beats. Consistency creates concentration. Repetition adds to the effect. Structurally the poem increases in intensity, as we move from verbs such as 'flow' and 'mark' in the first stanza to the more powerful emphatic verbs of 'curse', 'blasts' and 'blights' in the final stanza. This pattern is re-enforced by the examples of exploitation. These escalate from the crowd to the chimney sweeper to the soldier to the 'youthful harlot', a fact emphasized by Blake's use of the adjective 'most'.

Enjambment and caesura

Enjambment connects lines and stanzas; caesurae break lines up. The enjambment in the third stanza, for instance, underscores the causal link that Blake builds between the exploited and those who exploit them.

Look, for instance, at 'How the chimney…appalls' and then 'and the hapless…walls'.

In contrast the caesura in 'marks of weakness, marks of woe' creates a micro-pause between the two phrases, the effect of which is to make the reader hit that repeated noun 'marks' that little bit harder.

CONTEXTS

Literary

'London' is from **'SONGS OF EXPERIENCE'** (1792), the companion piece to his earlier 'Songs of Innocence'. The latter collection is darker, angrier and more sombre in tone. Blake was an idealist who wanted to see a better, fairer world. In many of these poems he analyses and criticises the harsh values of his society. Throughout the collection he protests against injustice and exploitation. He stands up as a champion of the poor and challenges the cruelty of those in power. In this enterprise Blake's spiritual guide was Christ whom he called 'Jesus, the imagination'.

Literary-historical: an age of revolutions

Blake's 'Songs of Innocence' poems generally focus on childhood and are celebratory and optimistic in tone; the 'Experience' poems are much angrier. This darkening of mood between the two may have been due to Blake's reaction to the French Revolution of 1789. Like other Romantic poets, initially Blake saw the revolution as a great uprising of the human spirit, a liberation of the masses from the corrupt and unjust powers of the State. But as time went on, news filtered through to England of appalling massacres carried out by the revolutionary forces. Over time it was becoming apparent that the French Revolution would result in one form of tyranny, that of the Monarchy, being replaced by another, that of the Masses.

VISUAL

Look at an image of the original design.

Blake's beautiful illustrations were an integral part of his poems. Many of the illustrations accompanying the 'Innocence' poems are rich, boldly coloured, sensual designs, presenting children playing in harmonious relation within exuberantly fertile images of nature. In contrast the palette of the 'Experience' is much narrower and gloomier, conjuring a shadow world, drained of colour, dominated by greys and blacks.

The characters in these images express suffering and misery. Boxed in by the borders of the page, they appear trapped in their oppressive worlds. It is interesting that Blake depicts himself as two figures in the illustration to 'London'. He is both the angelic child guide and the old man led through the circles of this particular depiction of hell. In other words he is both innocence and experience.

Significantly at the end of the poem the image of innocence has disappeared.

THE POEM CRUNCHED

Crunching is a way of focusing on the key words and ideas in a poem. To crunch a poem you have to reduce each line to just one word. Try this yourself and then see if you agree with my choices:

Wander – Chartered – Mark – Woe – Every – Cry – Every – Manacles - Chimney-sweeper – Church – Soldier – Palace – Midnight – Harlot - New-born - hearse

KEY REVISION

Themes

- The exploitation and brainwashing of the poor.

- The corruption and suffering of the city.

- The destruction of innocence.

Language

- Symbols of exploitation, such as the chimney sweeper.

- Insistent repetition of key images, words and phrases, such as 'in every' and 'mark'.

- Mainly simple, everyday words, no fancy terms or allusions - democratic language.

- Impassioned and angry emotive tone.

- Tight, almost claustrophobic sonic world.

Form and structure

- Four even, balanced quatrains. The lack of development perhaps suggesting stasis or entrapment even.

- Incantatory, spell like quality created by repetition in conjunction with tetrameter and cross rhyme scheme.

- Use of trochaic with docked final syllable adds to the intensity.

Contexts

- Example of Romanticism, a thematically and stylistically radical, anti-establishment form of literature, focused on generating a powerful emotional charge to jumpstart political and social change.

True or false? William Blake printed his own copies of his books.

MY NAME IS
OZYMANDIUS
KING OF KINGS

look
on my
works
ye mi
and
despa

Ozymandias

'I met a traveller from an antique land
Who said: `Two vast and trunkless legs of stone
Stand in the desert. Near them, on the sand,
Half sunk, a shattered visage lies, whose frown,
And wrinkled lip, and sneer of cold command,
Tell that its sculptor well those passions read
Which yet survive, stamped on these lifeless things,
The hand that mocked them and the heart that fed.
And on the pedestal these words appear --
"My name is Ozymandias, king of kings:
Look on my works, ye Mighty, and despair!"
Nothing beside remains. Round the decay
Of that colossal wreck, boundless and bare
The lone and level sands stretch far away.'

Percy Bysshe Shelley (1817)

CHARACTERS

Narrator

Use of the pronoun 'I' indicates the poem is written in the first person. Presumably this is the voice of Shelley himself. The poet introduces a 'traveller', and reports the traveller's statement. The traveller describes a scene in the desert, with a huge broken sculpture, and relates the inscription on its pedestal.

So we have in a sense three narrators:

1. The author of the poem

2. The first person voice

3. Words by or put in the mouth of the subject of the sculpture, Ozymandias - the Egyptian Pharaoh Ramasses II.

This little piece of recorded speech is related by the traveller, and hence enclosed within the traveller's narration. And all that the traveller says is related to us by the first speaker, the poet, and so enclosed by the poet.

This device of several enclosed narratives, rather like a Russian doll, means that Shelley can delineate the desert and the Pharaoh, their vastness and power, but at the same time control and enclose them as miniatures inside his field of powerful language, his poem.

Traveller

The traveller from 'an antique land' provides an exotic element to the poem and an implied contrast with the poet's more limited experience.

Romantic poets, such as Blake, Wordsworth and Shelley were drawn to solitary individuals who quested after knowledge, wisdom and understanding. This quest often took them to some sort of **SUBLIME** natural environment, such as a mountain range or a desert. It is characteristic of the Romantics to find wisdom far away from civilisation and the comforts of home.

Pharaoh

Ramasses is an emblem of autocratic political power: 'the sneer of cold command'.

He is presented as hubristic, meaning so full of his own self-importance that he is due a fall. Arrogance and vanity are demonstrated by his having a statue erected to himself on which he has the extraordinarily vain and foolish words, 'king of kings' engraved.

However magnificent and indomitable Ramasses thought himself, Shelley shows how puny his power is in relation to the vast power of nature and of time.

So Shelley's poem warns tyrants that however impregnable their position appears to be, they are in reality vulnerable. To the powerless, ordinary people this is a message of political hope.

To me, the image of the ruins of the Pharaoh's statue recalls images of

Saddam Hussein's statue being torn down. Power that seemed impermeable can be suddenly shaken and destroyed, and a new world order born.

The unnamed and unknown artist is a kindred spirit for the poet. Part of the poem's business is to assert and demonstrate the primacy and permanence of forms created by art over the more transient trappings of worldly power.

IMAGERY

What objects do we have in the poem? A traveller; the land; legs; desert; sand; a visage (face); a lip; a sculptor; a hand; a heart; a pedestal; Ozymandias; a wreck; sands.

The imagery gives the reader a sense of the exotic through the traveller, the antique land, and the extraordinary name, **'OZYMANDIAS'**. Shelley also includes images of desolation and destruction, such as the trunkless legs, shattered visage, decay, desert, sand and the wreck. Violence is also suggested generally through the wreckage, as well as specific verbs, such as 'shattered' and 'stamped'.

The scale of the statue is conveyed through the adjectives, 'vast' and 'colossal'. Yet this huge wreckage is dwarfed by the enormity of nature, here in its perhaps harshest form, the desert. The adjectival phrase 'boundless and bare' suggests the desert is both endless and endlessly featureless, a sense of an eternity of nothingness enhanced in the final line, 'the lone and level sands stretch away'. There is a suggestion here of the desert as time and the endless time of death. Even the most powerful dictator cannot escape the effects of time.

Visiting China a decade and a half ago, wandering around an art gallery,

I was struck by how the image was repeated in nearly every painting. The image was of plants, flowers, shrubs, mini trees in various versions, growing out of various-coloured and patterned vases. In each painting the plant seemed to be bursting out, overgrowing its container. Indeed many of the vases were painted with alarming cracks. Intrigued, I asked the curator the meaning of the **MOTIF**. He said that it was too dangerous to make political statements critical of the government in China. So the artists used a symbolic code. The containers represented state power, the plants the natural power of the people. The paintings were images of resistance and hope; some day the container would be broken and the plant would be free.

PATTERNS OF SOUND AND SENSE

The sound 'and' occurs fifteen times. That's a lot for a fourteen line poem, and that repetition of sound, coupled with its sense of going on, of continuing, adding, helps give the poem its drive and momentum.

Also the rhyme scheme, **ABAB ACDC EDEF EF** holds the poem tightly together, giving the reader an impression of something unified and complete. Notice how the first rhyme 'land' is passed from the first four line stanza, or quatrain, to the second, 'command', the seventh line, 'things' runs into the third quatrain, and the eighth, 'appear' continues into the final couplet.

Internal rhyme of 'round' and 'boundless' with the assonance of 'nothing', 'colossal' and 'lone' set up the finish by helping to slow and steady the reader. This change of tempo is reinforced by sonic qualities:

- The alliteration of 'boundless and bare' and 'lone and level'

- The dominant drawn out long 'o' and 'ow' sounds.

One interesting syntactical device Shelley employs in this poem is the use of two adjectives connected by 'and': 'vast and trunkless', 'boundless and bare', 'lone and level'. These give the reader a sense of full and yet qualified description, a double vision of the object described. It's an economical technique that helps give us the impression of a real landscape the poet is capturing rather than creating.

FORM AND STRUCTURE

It's a sonnet, although as we saw above the rhyme scheme isn't traditional. There is no obvious break in the pattern where you might expect the **VOLTA**, or 'turn'. The 'turn' is change in direction in a poem, a feature of traditional sonnets where, usually after the **OCTAVE**, there is a change or shift in emphasis or argument, or a new subject or angle is introduced. And indeed there is no turn in this sonnet. One thing that makes this poem so innovative is the way that instead of a neat argument, with a turn after line 8 and a flourish at the end, as with a conventional sonnet, the structure here is one of enclosure: three statements creating three little worlds within them. This delivers a tremendously powerful sense of unity, and allows the poet and the reader to play with and control scale in a seemingly effortless way.

Shelley is an expert at speeding up and slowing the reader down, so that the rhythm of the words underscores the meaning. For example:

- The line 'look on my words, ye Mighty, and despair' has only four stresses and so trips along quickly,   TUM ti – ti TUM   ti-TUM, ti-ti ti TUM.

- This creates a contrast with the following half line which is much slower, 'Nothing beside remains', TUM-ti ti-TUM ti-TUM.

Even though almost all of this poem is reported speech, and sounds natural enough, it still fits the sonnet form, without seeming in any way forced. That shows some considerable skill by Shelley. And though the lines would sound wrong read as iambic pentameter, that rhythm is there as part of the poem's deep undersong.

Enjambment and caesurae

ENJAMBMENT is the running of sentences over the line breaks; caesura is the splitting of lines with a pause. These two devices work together to run against the regular pattern of the rhyme. They help to convey the sense of a speaking voice, making the words sound more natural by reducing the emphasis at the end of each line. Look at the **END-STOPPED** lines: They come at the end of the octave:

- line 8, '…and the heart that fed'

- line 11, '…and despair'

- and in the final 'level' with its unequivocal full stop.

The effect is to lend greater emphasis to these particular rhyme words. The poem runs up in a long sentence to 'fed' a word that conveys how much the ordinary people relied on the 'heart', signifying emotions of the Pharaoh. Shelley wanted to emphasise 'despair' and 'away' for obvious reasons.

The caesurae in the final lines are particularly effective. The pauses after 'nothing beside remains' and 'colossal wreck' allow the absoluteness of the phrases to sink in, as well as suggesting momentarily empty or emptied space.

CONTEXTS

A Romantic poet and political idealist with strongly anti-establishment view,s who was writing at a time of political turbulence in Europe, Shelley is here asserting the more enduring power of art and artists over that of kings and pharaohs. What do you think? Who's more powerful, the Prime Minister or Muse? What is power? In what way is an artist/sculptor/poet powerful? Do they influence the world more or less than traditionally 'powerful' people?

Like his fellow Romantics Shelley also shows how the creations of man are made to seem minute when set against nature and the cosmic dimension of time.

THE POEM CRUNCHED

Obviously, this process will always be a personal one. This is just one possibility. Do it yourself and see where we agree and disagree. What have you spotted that I have not?

Antique – trunkless – desert – visage – sneer – sculptor – lifeless – mocked – pedestal - Ozymandias – despair – decay – wreck - sands

(One sign of this poem's greatness is the fact that it could be 'crunched' in many interesting ways – every single word tells).

KEY REVISION

Themes

- time and change, how all things are vulnerable to time

- life and art: Shelley suggests the supremacy of Art over political power

- power and its abuses: the Pharaoh is presented as vain and tyrannical

- the supreme, unanswerable power of nature

Language

- feels like story telling, ordinary speech patterns

- the two symbols of the desert and of the wreckage are central

- Shelley uses paired adjectives to create a sense of repetitive sameness

Form and Structure

- it's a Sonnet, usually a form used for love poems

- an unconventional rhyme scheme creates cohesion and a sense of unity

Contexts

- a revolutionary Romantic poem with a clear political message

- a warning to those in power; a promise to the powerless masses.

True of false? The poet Shelley was the husband of the novelist Mary Shelley, author of 'Frankenstein'.

The Charge Of The Light Brigade

I

Half a league, half a league,

Half a league onward,
All in the valley of Death
Rode the six hundred.
'Forward the Light Brigade!
Charge for the guns!' he said:
Into the valley of Death
Rode the six hundred.

II

'Forward, the Light Brigade!'
Was there a man dismayed?
Not though the soldier knew
Some one had blundered:
Theirs not to make reply,
Theirs not to reason why,
Theirs but to do and die:
Into the valley of Death
Rode the six hundred.

III

Cannon to right of them,
Cannon to left of them
Cannon in front of them
Volleyed and thundered;
Stormed at with shot and shell,
Boldly they rode and well,
Into the jaws of Death,
Into the mouth of Hell
Rode the six hundred.

IV

Flashed all their sabres bare,
Flashed as they turned in air
Sabring the gunners there,
Charging an army, while
All the world wondered:
Plunged in the battery-smoke
Right through the line they broke;
Cossack and Russian
Reeled from the sabre-stroke
Shattered and sundered.
Then they rode back, but not
Not the six hundred.

V

Cannon to right of them,
Cannon to left of them,
Cannon behind them

Volleyed and thundered;
Stormed at with shot and shell,
While horse and hero fell,
They that had fought so well
Came through the jaws of Death,
Back from the mouth of Hell,
All that was left of them,
Left of six hundred.

VI

When can their glory fade?
O the wild charge they made!
All the world wondered.
Honour the charge they made!
Honour the Light Brigade,
Noble six hundred!

Alfred, Lord Tennyson (1854)

CHARACTERS

Narrator

The poetic speaker created by Tennyson takes the form of a storyteller. However, the details and immediacy of the action seem as if experienced first-hand. This allows the poem to capture the daring energy of the attack: "boldly they rode and well" but also allows a comment upon the incident: "Honour the Light Brigade".

Soldiers

For a poem filled with soldiers and horses and cannons, there is a rather faceless quality to the entire affair.

Tennyson creates the types of sterile stereotypes that are necessary in all conflicts: Us and Them. The doomed brilliance of the British army is captured by the "**NOBLE SIX HUNDRED**", who seem to act as one entity.

The British soldiers embody the type of bravery that resulted in the largest empire since ancient Rome. Not only are they courageous and "noble" but they are unquestioning too: "Theirs not to reason why". We must remember that in Tennyson's day, such unquestioning obedience was to be praised. After the twentieth century's world wars and Vietnam, and with changing conceptions of the afterlife, such automatic and unquestioning obedience can be seen as foolish.

The Light Brigade epitomise speed, action and courage. Even their physical position, on horseback, elevates them symbolically above their enemies.

They are also associated with light in terms of God and goodness, with Tennyson here playing on their military classification.

Such positive associations, or connotations, are continued in the use of the verb "flashed" as the Light Brigade engage with the opposition. This association with light is slyly associated with right as they beam through the gloom of the "battery-smoke". This leads us logically to the "anti-Light" Brigade.

The enemy

Waiting for them at the other end of the "valley of Death" lie the enemy: the Russians and Cossacks. In contrast to the dynamic movement of the Light Brigade, they simply sit and wait, plotting the downfall of their noble adversaries. Even their weapon of choice tells us something of their dubious personalities: cannons versus sabres. We think: "surely there is no contest?"

Unfortunately for them, their smugness is about to be "shattered and sundered" by the rapid romantic sabres of the Light Brigade. The important verb "reeled" suggests enemy weakness in the face of overwhelming valour, despite the disastrous reality of the situation.

This discrepancy between the two fighting groups magnifies the feats of the Light Brigade whilst simultaneously belittling the fighting prowess of the Russians. Tennyson seems to be saying 'Go Britannia!' even when the British are going in the wrong direction to almost certain death.

There is also another group which we must consider; a group who are responsible for the event but not for the bravery. The commands of Lord Raglan create the opportunity for British fighting men to shine when confronted by high danger. However, how must we respond to the crucial verb "blundered"? We are now firmly located in that age-old wartime debate about who commands and who fights and, more importantly, who gets the glory of martial success.

Such debates stretch back as far as Homer's Iliad, where Achilles gets put out by his commander's (Agamemnon's) demands for the spoils of war. We remember Nelson and Churchill but who were the brave souls who actually did the fighting? Who knows? And that is partly the problem. For a more modern take on this tension between commanders and commanded, we need to look forward to the poetry of Siegfried Sassoon and Wilfred Owen.

IMAGERY

What key objects do we have in the poem? The Light Brigade; the valley of death; cannon fire; and the sabres.

We recognise the dominance of war imagery in the poem, but what is striking is the distinct lack of violence.

Contrasted with the gritty realism of the film Saving Private Ryan, this is poetry written in an age preoccupied with moral decency and glory; blood-splattered poetry would horrify rather than rouse Tennyson's reading public. Tennyson instead creates a very dramatic, almost cinematic, poem that focuses on movement. The driving force of the Brigade itself hurtles the reader into the midst of the battle, where Tennyson surrounds us with the sounds of war as opposed to the sights.

A real sense of forward momentum is generated by:

- verbs like "charge"

- the quasi-onomatopoeic "plunged"

- the metre

- the short line lengths

The first image of note is one where Tennyson makes it clear that this is not just some propagandist vehicle hurrahing the might of the British Military; he does do this but in a more sensitive way. When he proclaims that the Light Brigade are charging across "the valley of Death" we are left in no doubt whatsoever that destruction and loss are inevitable. In one way, of course, this makes the feat of the Light Brigade even more awe-inspiring (or stupid depending on your viewpoint). The valley of Death delivers a clear biblical resonance for Tennyson's Victorian audience as it borrows from Psalm 23: "Yea, though I walk through the valley of the shadow of death, I will fear no evil: for thou art with me; thy rod and thy staff they comfort me".

This imaginatively captures the physical space of the battle (a valley) but also manages to foreshadow the massive losses suffered by the Light Brigade.

The valley of death becomes almost a **MOTIF** that Tennyson uses throughout the poem, sometimes with interesting variations. The valley of death is repeated in stanza two and in stanza three is developed by linking death with hell itself. The valley of death becomes "the jaws of death", which personifies death itself as an all-consuming monster.

Tennyson cleverly links the "jaws" to the "mouth", but the mouth now belongs to hell rather than death itself. The gothic imagery suggests that the Light Brigade are food for the war machine itself.

Again, this particular coupling of "jaws of Death" and "mouth of hell" appears in the fifth stanza. This time, though, the Light Brigade retreat rather than charge into the terrible site of violence.

Another major source of effective imagery is the **AUDITORY IMAGERY** associated with the cannons that pepper the charging cavalry. The fact that cannons lined both sides of the valley as well as awaited them at the valley's end means that the Light Brigade were showered with deadly explosives from all angles. The booming cannons are captured through:

- The mere repetition of the word itself. The repetition of "cannon" at the start of stanza three mimics the sequential firing of the cannons.

- Repetition is employed again in the fifth stanza where the Light Brigade must face the firing cannons for the second time.

- Tennyson uses the storm imagery to capture the reality of the battlefield where he uses the verb "thundered". This captures not only the sound of the cannons but also strengthens the foreshadowing that all hell is about to break loose.

- Tennyson stretches this imagery by using another related verb: "stormed". The "shot and shell" from the cannons rains down on them in a storm of fire.

This fourth stanza also contains possibly the most important visual image in the poem, that of the Light Brigade's bright sabres.

Another example of repetition, the key word in the opening couplet is "flashed". The brightness of the metal sabres carries a positivity that contrasts with the dark cannons. It also intensifies the drama of Tennyson's cinematic treatment with the gleaming blades slicing through the oppressive enemy smoke. By using the hand-held light sabres (reminiscent of the light sabres of Star Wars), it elevates the British soldiers above their enemies. Despite the rather poor odds the Light Brigade see their foes "shattered and sundered".

This is interesting imagery itself as these verbs don't seem to suit actions suffered by humans but rather damage made to a faceless machine. Again, it is more difficult to sympathise with enemy robots being dismantled than seeing fellow human beings brutally sliced and diced in your name.

PATTERNS OF SOUND AND SENSE

For a poem about such a potentially emotive subject, Tennyson uses a quite simple approach. This simplicity avoids a hyperbolic, melodramatic treatment, which results in a much more considered response from the reader. He treads the line between the bravery and brutality of war very nimbly indeed. One of the key devices used is the age-old reliable repetition.

- The first example of this strategy of repetition is at the very start: "Half a league, half a league, / Half a league onward". Here the caesura (/) right in the middle of the opening line creates a sense of balance before the onward thrust of the second line, which has no such caesura.

- The repetition of the "half a league" also allows the narrator to present the point of view of the cavalrymen. There is no doubt as to whose side we are to be on. It also creates suspense as the moment of engagement must be waited for by both Light Brigade and reader. The first line also mimics the galloping of the charging horses in its sound effects (try it yourself and see what rhythm you construct). This metre never relents, which further adds to the poem's forward momentum.

- Tennyson also uses what might be termed a refrain, or a repeated section, at the end of each stanza. Again, to avoid exhaustion of effect he wisely introduces variation. Looking at the following excerpts we can see this refrain in action:

'Into the valley of Death / Rode the six Hundred'
'Into the valley of Death / Rode the six Hundred'
'Into the mouth of hell / Rode the six Hundred'
'Then they rode back, but not / Not the six Hundred'
'All that was left of them / Left of six Hundred'
Noble six hundred!'

While obviously the changes reflect the movement of the Light Brigade into and out of the battle, the inescapable entity is the Light Brigade itself. Note the clever use of caesura and word repetition as they charge back. Look at the dramatic pause after "Then they rode back", which allows the reader a brief moment of contemplation, which is coloured with sadness by the repetition of "not".

The same applies to the repetition of "left"; it is simple but devastating. What is also interesting is Tennyson's decision to concentrate on the collective, the six hundred, rather than an individual, which would have amplified the potential for sympathy from the reader.

At the end of the poem it is impossible to forget the six hundred, and not only that; due to his clever variations, what lingers is the last trumpeting line, celebrating the nobility of these fighting men.

There are only two really significant examples of **alliteration** in the poem and a similar number of assonances.

- Assonance and alliteration are used in "All the **wo**rld **wo**ndered". The importance of this message is so high that Tennyson repeats this in the final stanza.

- Another important example of alliteration arrives in stanza three, where the Light Brigade are "stormed at with **sh**ot and **sh**ell". Here the **sh** sounds mimic the noise of shells and buckshot slicing through the air all around the Light Brigade.

We have encountered repetition of syntax in the previous section. Of all the repeated phrases used by Tennyson, surely it is the "Honour...Honour" couplet in the final stanza that is most important.

This drives home the expected emotional response for the reader and it is hard to argue with the events as described in the poem. The other significant example is Tennyson's condensation of the soldier's duty on the battlefield: "Theirs not to make reply / Theirs not to reason why / Theirs but to do and die".

Whilst espousing the bravery of the men themselves for Tennyson's Victorian audience, it also leaves itself open to exploitation in the name of propaganda. Again, the First World War and the senseless losses suffered on both sides springs to a modern mind.

FORM AND STRUCTURE

The first thing notable about Tennyson's form is its irregularity.

There are 6 stanzas of varying lengths: 8 lines, 9 lines, 9 lines, 12 lines, 11 lines and finally 6 lines. Such irregularity is unusual, especially in Victorian poetry.

The rhyming scheme is a key part of the tension between regular and irregular in the poem. It is clearly irregular as it varies from stanza to stanza, but the reoccurrence of certain units in the stanzas lends familiarity and maybe the illusion of regularity. Visually the individual rhyme schemes look like this:

ABCBDDCB /
AABCDDDEC /
AAABCCDCB /
AAABCDDEDCFC /
AAABCCCDCEB /
AABAAB.

There is clearly variation in each stanza. Not one has the same rhyme scheme as another, but the occurrence of couplets and triplets is common, especially in stanzas 2 to 5. A strong connection between all the stanzas is Tennyson's imperfect rhyme with the word "hundred". He uses "blundered", "thundered" and "wondered" towards the beginning of each stanza with the "hundred" always the last word in the stanza.

Obviously, Tennyson repeatedly brings the attention of the reader to the "six hundred" but the three rhyme words can be seen to encapsulate the entire poem: the miscommunication, the peril, the glory.

The constant pulling between regularity and irregularity lends the poem a somewhat destabilised feel which mirrors the descent into chaos that confronts the Light Brigade. It could also link to the chaos of war trying to be controlled by military organisation. The emphasis on planning and strategy in military operations is key but can be undone simply by the pure haphazard nature of conflict itself.

Metre

Tennyson's use of metre is crucial. He chooses a very rare form called the dactylic dimeter. While sounding like a prehistoric animal long extinct, it simply means that Tennyson uses two heavy stresses [in bold] in each line in the following form:

> '*Half a league, half a league*

> *Half a league on ward*'

The stressed syllable is followed by two unstressed, which is called a **DACTYL** [/ X X]. What is the purpose of the dactyl? This metre mimics the sound of the thundering, charging horses. Try reading it for yourself. It may also connect to the booming of cannons. It is relentless throughout the entire poem but Tennyson does vary it. For example, in the refrain the last line only has five syllables but maintains the two stresses. In other instances he adds an extra syllable to the line to give seven syllables.

For example:

> '*In to the vall ey of Death*'

In this instance, there are 3 unstressed syllables after the stress on "vall". However, it could be argued that Death is also stressed, which might make more sense, so it becomes:

'_In_ to the _vall_ ey of _Death_'

This provides a greater sonic boom to the line and on such a key word too. The capitalisation of "Death" also increases the emphasis.

The structure of the poem is almost narrative driven.

Again, the structure is not symmetrical yet there is a clear reflection, albeit a distorted one. We see the charge into enemy lines mirrored by the retreat, but there is also the treatment of the fatal blunder in stanza two, which technically should start the poem. Tennyson instead chooses to start the poem **IN MEDIA RES**, as they are charging. This creates a real sense of excitement at the start instead, which may not have been achievable if sticking to a strictly chronological structure.

CONTEXTS

Biographical & Historical

The success of his 1842 Poems made Tennyson a popular poet and his appointment in 1850 as Poet Laureate established him as the most famous poet of the Victorian era. By then Tennyson, only 41, had written some of his greatest poetry, but he continued to write and to gain in popularity. In 1853, as the Tennysons were moving into their new house on the Isle of Wight, Prince Albert dropped in unannounced. His admiration for Tennyson's poetry helped solidify his position as the national poet. Queen Victoria later summoned him to court several times, and at her insistence he accepted his title, having declined it previously. Alfred, Lord Tennyson died on October 6, 1892, at the age of 83.

Socio-Historical

'The Charge of the Light Brigade' was a charge of British cavalry led by Lord Cardigan against Russian forces during the Battle of Balaclava on 25 October 1854 in the Crimean War. Lord Raglan, overall commander, had intended to send the Light Brigade to pursue and harry a retreating Russian artillery battery near the front line, a task well suited to light cavalry. Due to miscommunication at some level in the chain of command, the sabre-armed Light Brigade was instead sent on a frontal assault into a different artillery battery, one well-prepared with excellent fields of defensive fire. Although reaching the battery under withering direct fire and scattering some of the gunners, the badly mauled brigade was forced to retreat immediately, producing no decisive gains. 247 out of 637 men were killed or wounded. Blame for the miscommunication has remained controversial, as the original order from

Raglan itself was vague. Tennyson read about it in The Times and wrote the poem minutes later.

KEY REVISION

Themes

- Death and destruction are inescapable in battle.
- Military courage will ensure glory.
- Commanders must take full responsibility for the welfare of their men.

Language

- Simple, effective language that focuses on auditory imagery.
- Use of light imagery to symbolise the moral superiority of the British forces.
- Occasional use of alliteration for important messages: "All the world wondered".

Form and structure

- Six irregular length stanzas with echoing structural connection between them.
- Use of refrain, with variation.

- Metre used to capture galloping momentum/cannon fire.

Contexts

- Tennyson read about the tragedy in a newspaper report and wrote the poem immediately.

- Celebration of British military valour, even in defeat, in a time of growing empire means a celebration of imperialism itself.

True or False? Alfred Lord Tennyson had the longest beard of any of the famous English poets.

Glory be to God for
dappled things

Pied Beauty

Glory be to God for dappled things –
For skies of couple-colour as a brinded cow;
For rose-moles all in stipple upon trout that swim;
Fresh-firecoal chestnut-falls; finches' wings;
Landscape plotted and pieced – fold, fallow, and plough;
And áll trádes, their gear and tackle and trim.

All things counter, original, spare, strange;
Whatever is fickle, freckled (who knows how?)
With swift, slow; sweet, sour; adazzle, dim;
He fathers-forth whose beauty is past change:
Praise him.

Gerard Manley Hopkins (1877)

CHARACTERS

Narrator

Though Hopkins does not refer to himself in the poem in this way, he still creates a strong sense of a personal voice. This is achieved by a combination of the concentrated energy, the heightened tone, and the phrases that start and end the poem. As if spoken directly to us, the opening exclamatory phrase of the poem is completed in the command in the final line,

> 'Glory be to God...'
> ... 'praise him'

The narrative voice of the poem conveys wonder at the rich diversity of the world. Wherever the narrator looks he sees signs of beautiful 'piedness'. The title means a world of harmonious and various beauty; not a beautiful world made of pies! Think of 'pied' in the sense of 'magp**IE**', rather than 'pork' or 'apple pie'. He also finds this quality in nature and in the work of men, 'and all trades', 'all things'. Repetition three times of the simple adjective 'all' signifies the universality of this quality of 'piedness'.

Nature

Hopkins focuses on the sky, a cow, marks on trout, coal, chestnuts, finches' wings and an agricultural landscape. As big as the sky or a landscape, as small as a 'rose-mole' on a 'trout', in the water, the air or on land, nature is a consistent emblem of diverse beauty.

As a character nature is presented as passive, to be admired, visually beautiful and essentially 'double' in quality. Its creation and workings are also a little mysterious, 'who knows how?', a phrase which seems to be challenging emerging scientific explanations of nature, put forward in the Victorian era by Charles Darwin and others.

Hopkins is writing in the tradition of the Romantic poets, celebrating nature and its beauty, and finding within it the footprints of God.

However, where the Romantics were attracted to wild landscapes, Hopkins' version of nature is governed by pattern.

In other words, nature is celebrated for its neat orderliness; its energies are vibrant but contained and expressed as a pretty patterning of dots and stripes, like that of clothes. Consider for a moment what is excluded from this gentle, harmless and lovely vision of the natural world, such as nature's predatory violence - think of crocodiles, or its destructive power - earthquakes, and you'll see how selective and partial Hopkins is.

God

God in 'Pied Beauty' is to be glorified and worshipped. There are three reasons why:

1. God originates all the beauty of the world, 'he fathers-forth'.

2. He shares the same quality of 'beauty' with nature.

3. God's beauty is uniquely singular and constant; unlike everything else in the poem it is 'past change'.

The relationships

The poet celebrates the rich changeableness, or flux (see, for example 'fickle') as well as the variety of the world, specifically the quality of opposites it contains, such as sweetness and sourness. He is also entranced by the uniqueness of things that are 'original, spare, strange'. The ultimate individuality is, however, God - the creative source of all the rich variety of life. God is to be praised most highly for his uniquely eternal, unchanging quality.

IMAGERY

What objects do we have in the poem?

The sky, the cow, the rose-moles, trout, coal, chestnut, finches' wings, the landscape and tradesmen's equipment.

The imagery is concentrated in the first six lines or (**SESTET**) of the poem. The final four lines (**QUATRAIN**) are dominated by adjectives. But these are emptied of objects, other than the ultimate one, God.

The listing of multiple examples of piedness neatly exemplifies the variety the poet celebrates. It is as if Hopkins is pointing excitedly and saying 'look, look, God's beauty is everywhere'. The key qualities are:

1. The beauty of nature consists of harmonious opposites:

    *   The sky and cow are 'couple-colour' and 'brinded' (striped).

    *   The simile in the second line finds harmonious relation between the sky and a cow! (Sounds a bit unlikely, perhaps).

    *   The metaphor in the fourth implies the chestnut is so bright

it looks like a piece of coal on fire and vice versa.

- The 'rose-moles' are in 'stipple' (painted with dots).

2. This beauty also moves and changes:

- The trout 'swim', the chestnut 'falls', things are 'fickle', 'swift' and 'slow'.

- The feature of the finch on which Hopkins' chooses to focus is the 'wings'.

Landscape is praised both for containing opposites - the 'fallow' and the 'plough' - but also for its ordered pattern - 'plotted', 'pieced', 'fold'. Likewise the trades, made up of 'gear' and 'tackle', are neat and efficient, 'trim'.

So, despite their surface differences, the natural world, the agricultural world and the world of man are united by an underlying sense of harmonious good order and deep pattern.

PATTERNS OF SOUND AND SENSE

Repetition is a key poetic device for all poets, but it is especially important for Hopkins. It can fall into a few different categories: images, vocabulary, **SYNTAX**, sounds. The musical qualities of Hopkins' poetry are as critical as the meaning of the words.

We have already seen how the images repeat the same pattern of ideas about nature. We have noted how the adjective 'all' is used three times to convey the sense of universality.

Vocabulary

As well as a fondness for unusual words, such as 'brinded' and 'stipple', Hopkins often gives words new grammatical functions. He turns the adjective 'trim' into a noun and creates new words through **COMPOUNDING**.

- 'Couple-colour' - nouns becoming an adjective

- 'Rose-moles'   - adjective + noun = new noun

- 'Fresh-firecoal' - adjective + noun = new adjective

- 'Chestnut-falls' - noun + verb = noun

- 'Fathers-forth'   - noun + adverb = verb

To me, the compounding seems to neatly enact on a micro scale the idea of two things becoming one, and of flux (things changing).

Syntax

The poem is made up of just two sentences, each one forming a tightly packed list. In effect the first sentence says 'Glory be to God' for this, this, this, this and also for this. The second sentence neatly reverses the order, so that we have all the qualities first in a list of adjectives, before we arrive at the subject and cause, God.

Hence the poem starts and appropriately ends with God, all the teeming detail of the world enclosed by God.

Noticeably Hopkins uses repeated patterns of sentences and lists of features. Each line of the sestet starts with a feature of nature we should thank God for. Many of the lists of specific aspects of these fall into patterns of three, perhaps evoking the Holy Trinity:

- 'fresh-firecoal chestnut-falls; finches' wings'

- 'fold, fallow, and plough'

- 'gear, tackle and trim'

- 'swift, slow; sweet, sour; adazzle, dim'.

Hopkins' poetry is famous for its compression and intensification of spoken language. He squeezes out dull old functional words:

- 'for skies that are of couple-colour' contracts to 'skies of couple-colour',

- 'all things that are counter,' becomes the more dynamic 'all things counter',

- 'landscape that is plotted and pieced' is intensified as 'landscape, plotted and pieced'.

SOUND EFFECTS

The central theme of harmonious variety is enacted in the poem through the running chains of sounds.

Words, images and phrases echo, chime, ping and ring off each other, creating a richly textured and intensely musical, euphonic sound world.

Major sonic effects include:

Alliteration

Just in the sestet there is:

- '**G**lory be to **G**od'
- '**c**ouple-**c**olour…**c**ow'
- '**f**resh-**f**irecoals…**f**alls; **f**inches''
- '**p**lotted and **p**ieced…**p**lough'
- '**f**old, **f**allow'
- '**t**rades…**t**ackle and **t**rim'

From this it is apparent that each line has a dominant alliterative sound pattern knitting the line together.

Assonance, or vowel rhyme

- 'c**ou**ple-c**o**lour'
- 'r**o**se-m**o**les'

(Notice too how the full rounded sound of these two words contrasts with the quicker, thinner, lighter, 'finches' wings')

- 'co**u**nter', 'pl**ou**gh'
- 'str**a**nge', 'tr**a**de'
- 'th**i**ngs...sw**i**m...w**i**ngs...tr**i**m...f**i**ckle...sw**i**ft...d**i**m...h**i**m'

Consonantal rhyme

- '**p**lotted...**p**ieced'
- '**s**wift...**s**weet'

Internal rhyme and rhymes across lines

- 'all...fall...all'
- 'in...swim'
- 'follow...slow...know'

One internal rhyme sounds runs through the poem like a golden thread:

- 'dapple...couple...rosemole...stipple...firecoal...tackle... fickle...
- freckled...adazzle'

Check and you'll find that almost no word in the poem remains unconnected from the mesh of sound to at least one other.

This interconnectedness of the words and sounds, as with the imagery and the syntax, implies an underlying unity, pattern and coherence in the world.

FORM AND STRUCTURE

Metre

Traditionally in well-made poems, the poet keeps to one dominant metre. Try scanning 'Pied Beauty' and you'll find the pattern becomes increasingly irregular:

> 'Glory be to God for dappled things'
>
> TUM-ti, TUM-ti, TUM-ti, TUM-ti, TUM

So the first line has five stresses, with the pattern stress, unstress. The technical term for this is **TROCHAIC PENTAMETER**.

> 'For skies of couple-colour as a brinded cow'
>
> Ti-TUM, ti-TUM, ti-TUM, ti-ti, ti-TUM, ti-TUM

The second line reverses the pattern, to a mostly regular **IAMBIC** pentameter.

In the third, fourth and fifth lines the pattern thickens or swells, with at least one extra stress. There is also no dominant pattern of either iambic or trochaic to tether the lines:

'**Lands**cape **plott**ed and **pieced** – **fold**, **fall**ow, and **plough**'

TUM-ti, TUM-ti, ti-TUM, TUM-ti- TUM-ti, ti-TUM.

Hopkins wanted to do away with a regular beat. He had radical ideas about metre and developed his own metrical rules, which he called 'sprung rhythm'. He found these conventional metres limiting and mechanistic, so he invented something looser, more adaptable and more varied. In his 'sprung rhythm' the poet could use as many, or as few, unstressed syllables in a line as he wanted, so long as each line had the same number of stressed syllables. %%%

The effect is to flex the form of the poem, to fill it with more stresses, so that it seems overloading and bulging, full to brimming. %%%

So the poem's form embodies the idea of the rich fertility and variety of nature.

Enacting the sense of energy and change in the poem, the irregularity of the metre also suggests spontaneous thought poured out in passion. Though the surface pattern of each line changes, however, the more regular number of stresses and the regular pattern of full rhymes again imply that underpinning coherent design.

Rhyme Scheme

'Pied Beauty' has a technically demanding scheme as there are only four rhyme sounds: ings, ow, im, ange. The 'im' and 'ow' rhyme neatly make a sonic link between the two stanzas. The use of full masculine rhymes and consonantal rhyme ring off each other to make the poem's soundworld harmonious and melodic.

Although Hopkins did not break through to writing **FREE VERSE** (poetry freed from metre, without a set number of stresses in a line, invented in the twentieth century), his metrical experiments took him pretty close and show how radically experimental and ahead of his time he could be.

Stanzas

'Pied Beauty' is what Hopkins called a '**CURTUL SONNET**', a sonnet condensed from the conventional 14 to just 10 and a half lines. The poet sought to keep the same sense of proportion as in the original form, but shrunk the 8/6 down to a 6/4 pattern of stanzas, so that the content would appear to be bursting from its constraints.

Conventionally, in a sonnet the last line of the octave is called a **VOLTA**. The octave sets out a situation or question to which the sestet is the response. In Hopkins' sonnet the quatrain serves a different function; drawing out and emphasising the idea articulated in the sestet.

Enjambment and caesurae

Enjambment connects lines and stanzas; caesurae break them up. Hopkins employs both devices to suggest superficial separation, and the profound interconnectedness we have already noted underpins various aspects of the poem. Caesura is used in the line 'fresh firecoals, chestnut falls; finches' wings' where there seems little in common in terms of meaning to connect fire coals to a little bird's wings. The line is woven together though through the alliteration. So we have again separation and connection.

Many of the lines are **END-STOPPED** with each line of the sestet, for instance, dealing with a separate subject – skies, rose-moles, fire coals, landscape, trades. In addition to the sonic links working across these lines, the similar sentence structures connect them too.

CONTEXTS

Literary: Convention vs. eccentricity

A Catholic priest as well as a poet, Hopkins was unlike other Victorian poets. In particular his experiments with metre and syntax, alongside their concentrated musical intensity, made his poems original, but also difficult and obscure. Even his best friend and lifelong correspondent, the poet laureate, Robert Bridges, warned Hopkins that the eccentricities of his style ruined his work.

For Hopkins, though, his poetic style was the expression of his individuality; the style of his poetry expressed the same original, spare, strange qualities in nature that he celebrates in 'Pied Beauty'.

Socio-historical: The Victorian Age

Written in 1877, Hopkins' poem presents a pastoral idyll to set against the reality of rapidly industrialising cities. As a poet and as a priest, Hopkins was appalled at the squalor of modern cities and the devastating effects working conditions had on the lives of the workers, especially their spiritual lives. In some ways too the poem can be see as a challenge or answer to scientific explanations of nature.

THE POEM CRUNCHED

This process will always be a personal one. This is just one possibility. Do it yourself and see where we agree and disagree. What have you spotted that I have not?

Glory - Couple-colour – Stipple – Wings – Landscape – Trades – Strange - Fickle - Sour- him

KEY REVISION

Themes

- Celebrating the diversity of nature as evidence of God's presence on earth.

- A celebration of God as uniquely creative, unchanging and immutable.

- Implicitly challenges science and Darwin's theory of evolution.

Language

- Self-consciously poetic, heightened and intensified.

- Hopkins cuts out function words and uses long packed lists.

- Sound connects words and images, within and across lines and stanzas, forming a rich harmonious musical texture.

- The tone shifts from rapturous to more reflective, pious and celebratory.

Form and structure

- An unusual type of sonnet, compressed and intensified, but keeping to a similar ratio.

- Rather than following the conventional question and answer, call and response, pattern, the quatrain makes explicit the idea implied in the opening sestet.

Contexts

- Though this is a Victorian poem it rejects the contemporary industrial world to find beauty, meaning and God in nature.

- Defiantly spiritual, the pastoral is intensified and given a modern feel through original metre and compressed syntax.

True of False? When he became a Jesuit priest, Hopkins threw all his early poems into a fire and burnt them.

and Mourners to and fro

i felt a Funeral
in my Brain

I Felt a Funeral In My Brain

I felt a Funeral, in my Brain,
And Mourners to and fro
Kept treading – treading – till it seemed
That Sense was breaking through –

And when they all were seated,
A Service, like a Drum –
Kept beating – beating – till I thought
My Mind was going numb –

And then I heard them lift a Box
And creak across my Soul
With those same Boots of Lead, again,
Then Space – began to toll,

As all the Heavens were a Bell,
And Being, but an Ear,
And I, and Silence, some strange Race
Wrecked, solitary, here –

And then a Plank in Reason, broke,
And I dropped down, and down –
And hit a World, at every plunge,
And Finished knowing – then –

Emily Dickinson (1861, published 1896)

CHARACTERS

Whilst the poem is dominated by the first person narrator relating their experiences to the reader, there is a distinct opposition in the poem between the singular "I" and the plural "they."

Narrator

The poetic speaker in this poem is a first person narrator i.e. "I". With a first person narrator, the poem becomes a very immediate, personal experience. In this case, this gives the poem a confessional tone, with the first person narrator confiding in the reader. The narrator in "I Felt a Funeral in my Brain" plays an active yet also curiously passive role in the poem.

This lends the poem a feeling of helplessness or powerlessness; the narrator describes their emotional responses to things done to them by others.

Looking at the verbs associated with the narrator gives us an indication of what is happening in the poem:

I: "felt" "thought" "heard" "wrecked" "dropped"

These verbs emphasise the personal nature of this experience, which makes the poem a record of intense feeling. There is a clear prioritisation of sensual experience implied in the verbs "felt" and "heard." In this case "felt" is more an emotional feeling than a physical sensation.

"Wrecked" and "dropped" are very dynamic verbs, which suggest a form of destruction or dangerous experience. By the end of the poem the narrator seems to have become an emotional wreck, but mysteriously the cause for such an emotional catastrophe remains unclear. The use of present tense also conveys a sense of recording this experience as it happens, which gives the poem a sense of excitement.

Mourners

The fact that "they" are "Mourners" suggests that something has been lost and must be grieved for.

Despite the intense emotion that grief entails, these Mourners and the narrator seem detached from one another. The mourners are obviously an intrusion into the mental world of the narrator and seem to be a collective force of disturbance in the poem. They are responsible for the overwhelming noise that assaults the sense of the narrator with their ceaseless "treading – treading –" in their "Boots of Lead".

Rather than bring comfort through ritual, these intrusive mourners bring distress and breakdown.

IMAGERY

What objects do we have in the poem? All the paraphernalia of funerals, various noises and an ear.

Dickinson is a master of unusual and highly eccentric imagery. She often married abstract concepts to peculiarly physical objects in some of her other poems, such as "Hope is the thing with feathers" and "My life had stood a loaded gun." In the latter she uses an extended metaphor, where the funeral represents a mental disturbance or mental collapse in the narrator's mind. The connecting concept between the narrator's experience and the funeral must be loss.

While funerals revolve around the loss of a person, i.e. a bodily loss, Dickinson seems to be describing a loss of personality or a loss of control.

All the features of a funeral are present in the poem: the "Mourners," the "Service," the "Box," or coffin, the "Bell" and, finally, the lowering of the coffin into the ground. Dickinson, then, follows the actual chronology of a funeral to describe the breakdown suffered by the narrator.

This is a poem dominated by the transmission of sounds and the receiving of these sounds.

For a chronicle of a mental breakdown, Dickinson chooses unusually sensual language (imagery that provokes an emotion) to try to relate to this experience. How can the narrator feel a funeral in their brain and what might that actually feel like?

It seems to suggest unwanted intrusion.

It is also a physical response to an overwhelming mental episode. The repetition of "treading – treading – " reinforces the invasiveness of the funeral goers and it builds to an almost unbearable pitch.

The **MOTIF** of overwhelming noise is continued in the second stanza, where Dickinson uses a simile to equate the service with a drum. From the relentless pounding of drums in the second stanza Dickinson increases the dramatic tension in stanza three. A very gothic "creak" (presumably of the coffin lid or floorboard) ultimately leads to a complete cosmic upheaval:

> *"Space – began to toll // As all the Heavens were a Bell."*

Dickinson equates existence with being "but an Ear" – merely a tiny receiver dealing with the noise of the entire universe.

Such pressure on the narrator's mind cannot continue indefinitely. Dickinson ends her poem with a dramatic snap. The "Plank" that breaks under the unbearable load of existence relates explicitly to "Reason." Logic or reason is essential in dealing with reality but here it is destroyed under the weight of some unspecified trauma. The final "plunge" into darkness symbolises the descent into mental breakdown. The end of the poem ends literally with the ending either of life itself or of mental stability. While the poem could be seen as an account of complete mental breakdown, it could also be a comment on Christian religion. Religion is a prominent aspect of the poem but the bleak isolation of the poem's end does not correspond with the comfort of an afterlife at all.

PATTERNS OF SOUND AND SENSE

Dickinson's poetry is very economical in its style. She concentrates maximum meaning into minimum expression. Her style is deceptively simple when it comes to patterns of sound as a result.

The first and most obvious form of sound pattern in this poem is repetition of words. This is found in the first two stanzas where Dickinson describes the "treading – treading –" of the "Mourners" and the "beating – beating –" of the "Drum". Both of these serve to intensify the experience being described by the narrator. The second type of repetition found is in the ABCB rhyme scheme. Dickinson employs **MASCULINE RHYME** here, i.e. all on stressed syllables, which gives the poem a strong echo pattern throughout, i.e. "Soul" and "toll". However, it is significantly weak at the end of the poem: "down" and "then."

Perhaps the weakness of the rhyme at the end signifies the loss of strength to go on.

Another important sound effect at a poet's disposal is **ONOMATOPOEIA**. In this poem, there is an effective example which adds significantly to the heavy aural aspect of the poem, namely the 'gothic "creak" across my soul'. %%%

This has an interesting connotation. Thanks to horror films, the modern reader will connect creaking to the opening of doors [and coffins, vampire slayers], which usually signifies the intrusion of a threatening and unwanted presence.

Given the condensed style of the poem, the more subtle sound patterns are few and far between. The penultimate stanza is quite sound rich:

'As all the Heavens were a Bell,
And Being, but an Ear,
And I, and Silence, some strange Race
Wrecked, solitary, here – '

Dickinson employs effective **ASSONANCE** here and uses different combinations of vowel sounds to create varying sound patterns. Firstly, there are the broad "e" sounds of "th**E** h**EA**v**E**ns w**E**re a B**E**ll", which contrast with the sharper, narrower "e" sounds in the next line "B**EI**ng but an **EA**r". Then there is a return to broad vowels with the "i" sounds in "And, I and Silence". All in all she uses a variation of broad and narrow vowel repetition that may reflect the confusion of emotions felt by the narrator. Certainly, the profusion of sibilance in "**S**ilence, **S**ome **S**trange Ra**C**e" creates an eerie whispering noise that is punctured by the sharp, fricative of "wre**CK**ed" in the next line, again suggesting disharmony and conflict.

FORM AND STRUCTURE

For a poem that explores what it feels like to completely lose control, it has a surprisingly controlled and regular form.

Dickinson uses five very regular quatrains to chronicle the narrator's journey into oblivion. The quatrain with the rhyme scheme ABCB and alternating 8/6 syllable lines is a form that she uses often in her poetry and is also common in church hymns and folk ballads. This makes it a particularly apt form for "I Felt a Funeral in my Brain," with its focus on religious ritual.

However, irregularity and momentary loss of control can be seen. Firstly, there is the rhyme scheme itself. While very strong in places, **"Drum"** and **"numb"**, the final stanza displays a weak half rhyme, **"down"** and **"then"**. In fact, it is so weak that it may be argued that that any chance of regular rhyme has been destroyed by the overwhelming content of this final apocalyptic stanza. Dickinson also employs irregularity of metre in the poem. She uses a traditional **iambic metre** and alternating between **tetrameter** (four stressed syllables) and **trimeter** (three stressed syllables) throughout the poem, a metrical pattern which makes this a strange sort of **ballad**. For example:

'I **felt** / a **Fune** / ral, **in** / my **Brain**,

And **Mour** / ners **to** / and **fro**'

However, at the end of the fourth stanza she builds tension by overloading the number of stressed syllables.

'And **I**, / and **Sil** / ence, **some** / **strange Race**

Wrecked, sol / i **tar** / y, / **here** –'

Where there would be four stresses in a tetrameter, there are now five; where normally three stresses would be found in a trimeter, now there are four.

The lines seem to be struggling to contain the huge emotions experience by the narrator.

In her handwritten manuscripts, Dickinson uses dashes quite unpredictably, but how do they influence the meaning of the poem? Every stanza in "I Felt a Funeral in my Brain" has at least one dash. Some of these make logical sense within the stanza, i.e. the "Drum - / Kept beating - beating – till I thought". The first dash acts as an almost unnecessary endstop but the "Drum" is clearly linked to the "beating" in the next line. In contrast, the two dashes in the middle of the line act as dramatic caesurae, breaks in the movement of the verse. They make the reader pause as Dickinson visually draws significance to the "beating" the narrator must endure and then amplifies this through repetition of the word itself. A particularly good example of the drama that can be condensed into a dash comes in the final line of the third stanza where "Space – began to toll". The dash here creates a pause where there is no logical need for one.

It seems to suggest that the narrator cannot comprehend the enormity of what is experienced, almost as if they are searching for the right word to describe their experiences.

In other instances, particularly at the end of a stanza, the dash signifies an implied breaking off as if the narrator's thoughts are broken off, or fragmented.

THE POEM CRUNCHED

Obviously, this process will always be a personal one. This is just one possibility. Do it yourself and see where we agree and disagree. What have you spotted that I have not?

Funeral – Mourners – Treading – Breaking – All – Drum – Beating – Numb – Box – Creak – Boots – Space – Heavens – Being – Strange – Wrecked – Broke – Dropped – World – Finished

CONTEXT

In 1830, Emily Dickinson was born in Amherst, Massachusetts. Throughout her life, she seldom left her house and visitors were scarce. The people with whom she did come in contact, however, had an enormous impact on her thoughts and poetry. She met and fell in love with the Reverend Charles Wadsworth, in 1854. He left for the West Coast shortly after a visit to her home in 1860, and this coincided with a huge outpouring of poetry in the years that followed. While extremely prolific as a poet she was not publicly recognised during her lifetime. Dickinson's poetry reflects her loneliness. The speakers of her poems generally live in a state of want. Her poems are also marked by the intimate recollection of inspirational moments which suggest the possibility of happiness. Dickinson died in Amherst in 1886.

KEY REVISION

Themes

- death, madness and loss of control
- the isolation of the individual in society
- the importance of ritual in coping with suffering

Language

- language of the funeral ritual
- domination of sound imagery
- tone of frustration and fear
- overwhelming cosmic sound imposed upon the individual listener

Form and structure

- five quatrains with ABCB rhyme scheme, like a church hymn
- chronological structure follows funeral procession and ends with complete oblivion
- corruption of dominant iambic metre to create high tension
- use of capitalisation and dashes to create dramatic pauses

Contexts

- her personal crisis of abandonment by impossible love
- Dickinson's puritan upbringing and personal fascination with death

True or false? Emily Dickinson didn't have a single poem published in her life time.

i took the one
less travelled,
and that has
made all the
difference

The Road Not Taken

Two roads diverged in a yellow wood,
And sorry I could not travel both
And be one traveler, long I stood
And looked down one as far as I could
To where it bent in the undergrowth;

Then took the other, as just as fair,
And having perhaps the better claim
Because it was grassy and wanted wear,
Though as for that the passing there
Had worn them really about the same,

And both that morning equally lay
In leaves no step had trodden black.
Oh, I marked the first for another day!
Yet knowing how way leads on to way
I doubted if I should ever come back.

I shall be telling this with a sigh
Somewhere ages and ages hence:
Two roads diverged in a wood, and I,
I took the one less traveled by,
And that has made all the difference.

Robert Frost (1916)

CHARACTERS

The narrator

The verbs associated with the narrator are:

- I could not*

- I stood*, looked*

- Took*

- I marked*

- I doubted* if I should (conditional tense)

- I shall (formal future tense) be telling

- I took*

Despite this poem being about the 'journey' of life, the verbs associated with the narrator are rather hesitant. Most* are in the past tense and these are static, negative and suggest **FATE** as well as **FREE WILL**.

The wood and the roads

The wood and the two roads might be considered to be 'setting' but they play so important a role in the poem that it is worth regarding them as characters in the drama.

Look at the adjective used to describe the wood. It is a 'yellow' wood and the use of the colour is suggestive. Is yellow being used here in the (American) sense of cowardly? If it is, then is the narrator's journey an attempt to escape? The 'yellow' wood might also be seen as a comment on the season. Is it autumn? If so, the time of year might be relevant to the situation of the narrator; there could be a suggestion that he will not be able to 'come back.'

Whatever the meaning of 'yellow' the colour is unsettling. It is not fresh and green and the word might be seen as rather sickly.

A popular reading of the poem tends to stress the difference between the two roads, but crucially one line suggests they are 'really about the same'. So, does the time spent making a decision make any difference when there will always be a 'road NOT taken'? It could be argued that the appearance of decision-making is just a charade. Really his decision was arbitrary; he had no reason to choose one path over another. It was only afterwards that he rationalised it. Unsettlingly, Frost implies that this is how we all make decisions in our lives.

The fact that the two roads 'diverge' is striking. The verb suggests the increasing impossibility of ever returning, an idea which is developed with the simple phrase 'way leads on to way'. This shows the complexities of life and gives a strong geographical sense of the journey. At the same time it makes the likelihood of returning ever more remote.

IMAGERY

What objects do we have in the poem? Clearly there are the wood and the two roads. The poem can also be read in terms of time. So, the poem also works on a literal and a figurative level, which adds complexity to a seemingly accessible and conversational work.

Let's start with the literal and figurative readings of the poem. The poem could be about a time when the narrator took a certain route in a wood. Here the experience of choosing a route through the woods is transformed into something far beyond the mundane by means of **ALLEGORY**. Frost is talking about the choice of path and this decision can be seen as a life choice as well as a navigational puzzle.

The wood was discussed in the previous section as a character. What associations might we have with woods? The narrator in the poem is alone and being in the woods isolates him. The wild wood is a place of folklore and myth where all sorts of things might happen (think about Red Riding Hood or Mirkwood in 'The Hobbit'). A wood is also a place where it is hard to see clearly.

Consequently we can see the wood as a place that is not entirely comforting and could even be threatening.

Like the wood, the two roads cropped up in the earlier section. Again, it is worth thinking about the way Frost presents these roads. The verb 'diverged' presents the narrator with a stark and absolute choice and the notion of 'the crossroads' has a powerful resonance in American folklore (just look up the life story of the blues guitarist Robert Johnson for a particularly exciting 'crossroads' story) The line,

'And both that morning equally lay / in leaves no step had trodden black'

seems to indicate that once someone (the narrator) does step down that road, the leaves will be 'trodden black'.

The colour imagery suggests that this spur of the moment decision, made in the yellow wood may have dark consequences. This is linked with the word 'sigh' in the final stanza which hints at disillusionment, but could also be a sigh of relief.

The unsettling quality of the road not taken is shown in the phrase 'where it bent in the undergrowth'. The verb 'bent' gives the road a sinister action and suggests straying off the 'straight and narrow'. The fact that the road bends into the 'undergrowth' is also rather unnerving and the word hints at concealment.

The narrator 'takes the other' which is 'just as fair' (though note, crucially not 'fairer') despite the negative descriptions of the other path. This could be seen as a use of irony as the chosen route is similarly threatening.

The timeframe is more complicated than it first appears and works best on a time line; he has realised that his decision is important and anticipates a future where he will 'sigh'.

- The decision made in the wood -- Verbs in past tense

- The time the narrator is speaking -- I Shall be telling this... (anticipates future)

- The future -- ages and ages hence'

The poet knows he will be 'telling' his story which seems to place him as a character in his own narrative.

PATTERNS OF SOUND AND SENSE

Robert Frost's verse is accessible and conversational. He wanted to make poems out of ordinary words, following the rhythms of a spoken voice. He also tells stories which are easy to visualise. Despite being precise in terms of setting, his poems have an appealing universality about them. The narrator orders the words so that the setting is made clear before placing himself in that setting.

The first thing to notice is that the 'voice' of the narrator is highly distinctive in terms of **SYNTAX**. Pick out all the examples where the word order is strange or 'quirky'. The narrator also uses conversational links such as 'and', 'though', 'because'.

There is careful use of repetition in this poem. This is because he knows that '**WAY** leads on to **WAY**' and he doubts if he will 'ever come back'. Certain phrases are also repeated 'Two roads diverged.' The first time they diverge in a 'yellow' wood but by the time he has started to think about the future, it has become just 'a wood'. Its colour is no longer important; what matters is that this is where his decision was made. There is also a repetition of the word 'I' in the final stanza. This tiny feature works on a number of levels:

- The 'I' is positioned at the end of line three of the stanza which immediately signals its importance – it forms part of the rhyme scheme.

- BUT it also comes at the very end of the clause 'and I' which seems to hint at his insignificance.

- The 'I' is repeated at the start of the fourth line. This gives a stuttering effect and conveys a sense of uncertainty and ambiguity.

- The sound of the second 'I' also forms an internal rhyme with 'by', consolidating the narrator's place in the narrative.

FORM AND STRUCTURE

Metre

Scan the first stanza and you will find that there are four stressed beats in each line. Generally speaking the poem is written in **IAMBIC TETRAMETER** but there are extra (unstressed) beats which provide a degree of freedom and allow Frost to maintain speech rhythms of a conversational voice.

'Two **roads**/ di**verged**/ in a **yell**/ow **wood**,

And **sor**/ry **I** /could not **tra**/vel **both**

And **be**/ one **tra**/veller, **long**/ I **stood**

And **looked**/ down **one**/ as **far**/ as I **could**

To **where**/ it **bent**/ in the **un**/der**growth**;'

Here the stresses are emboldened and the feet with the 'extra' are in lines one, two and five. This allows Frost the flexibility to write in a naturalistic way. At the same time it enables him to stick mainly to **IAMBIC TETRAMETER**, the metre of songs and spells.

Stanzas and rhyme scheme

The poem consists of four stanzas of five lines (**QUINTAINS**) with four beats. The rhyme scheme of the poem is abaab.

The cross rhymed lines give a sense of movement and progress, but the enclosure of the rhyming couplets in lines three and four (in an envelope scheme) might be seen as a device by which Frost is able to convey a sense of entrapment and inevitability.

The rhymes are **MASCULINE** (the rhymes fall on the stressed beats) with the exception of the feminine final line.

This famously enigmatic last line is left unresolved by means of this device. The reader is left uncertain about what 'difference' has been made, and whether crucially Frost made a good or bad decision.

Stanzas of five lines are also unsettling. Four lines suggest balance, regularity and completeness. The extra line works like an unbalancing afterthought. The stanzas seem to come to a conclusion, only for there to be another extra line.

This coming to a seeming conclusion and then undercutting it with doubt embodies in form the main theme of the poem.

Enjambment and caesurae

Enjambment is used to maintain the flow of **COLLOQUIAL** speech. It is tempered by the use of caesurae which are like the tiny hesitations a speaker might make as he searches for the right word. So, Frost takes us into the moment of writing the poem and creates an intimacy between himself and the reader.

THE POEM CRUNCHED

Obviously, this process will always be a personal one. This is just one possibility. Do it yourself and see where we agree and disagree. What have you spotted that I have not?

Diverged – sorry – one – far – undergrowth – took – perhaps – because

KEY REVISION

Themes

- life as a journey
- decisions and their impact on the future. Frost suggests that most of the choices we make are pretty random, based more on whim or chance than on a rational consideration of the alternatives
- fate and free will

Language

- colloquial, confessional, conversational language which creates a sense of intimacy between narrator and reader

- Frost uses simple, everyday language which emphasises the universality of the decision making process

- relaxed tone is at odds with the anticipation of an unsatisfactory future

- determinedly plain-speaking and 'unpoetic', Frost doesn't use obviously fancy elaborate poetic language or technique. The central metaphor of life as a journey is a common one

Form and Structure

- Four **QUINTAINS** with an abaab rhyme scheme. The first two lines in each stanza suggest movement, but the aa couplet suggests indecision (and/or entrapment), an inability to move on from the impact of the original decision.

- The **IAMBIC TETRAMETER** is flexed slightly which allows the 'flow' of the conversation and is mimetic of the 'hiccups' in life. A feminine final rhyme underscores the enigmatic final line.

Context

- An American poem focusing on one extended metaphor, or **CONCEIT**, but conveyed in a 'homespun', as if spoken, voice.

- Frost tried his hand at many careers before becoming a successful poet in his forties. A teacher, farmer, millhand, newspaper reporter, he found it difficult to settle to any one thing & moved his family from America to England in 1914.

- At the time of writing, Frost's English friend, the poet Edward

Thomas, was deciding whether to enlist in the British Army.

True or False? Robert Frost was 40 years old when he had his first book of poems published.

Dulce et Decorum Est

Bent double, like old beggars under sacks,
Knock-kneed, coughing like hags, we cursed through sludge,
Till on the haunting flares we turned our backs
And towards our distant rest began to trudge.
Men marched asleep. Many had lost their boots
But limped on, blood-shod. All went lame; all blind;
Drunk with fatigue; deaf even to the hoots
Of tired, outstripped Five-Nines that dropped behind.
Gas! Gas! Quick, boys! – An ecstasy of fumbling,
Fitting the clumsy helmets just in time;
But someone still was yelling out and stumbling,
And flound'ring like a man in fire or lime . . .
Dim, through the misty panes and thick green light,
As under a green sea, I saw him drowning.
In all my dreams, before my helpless sight,
He plunges at me, guttering, choking, drowning.
If in some smothering dreams you too could pace
Behind the wagon that we flung him in,
And watch the white eyes writhing in his face,
His hanging face, like a devil's sick of sin;
If you could hear, at every jolt, the blood
Come gargling from the froth-corrupted lungs,
Obscene as cancer, bitter as the cud
Of vile, incurable sores on innocent tongues,
My friend, you would not tell with such high zest

To children ardent for some desperate glory,
The old Lie; Dulce et Decorum est
Pro patria mori.

Wilfred Owen (1917)

CHARACTERS

Narrator

The verbs associated with the narrator begin with the first person plural pronoun 'we':

- we cursed

- we turned

- we trudge

This is a collective, group experience. In these conditions the soldiers are not differentiated by rank (officer or private) or by class; they are all in this horrific situation together, respond in the same way and suffer equally. The poet does not set himself apart.

The focus shifts from the group to the individual experience when Owen employs the first person singular in the line 'As under a green sea I saw him drowning'. The subject of the verb changes to the 3rd person in the line that follows:

'He plunges at me'

The change to the personal pronouns emphasises Owen's role as a witness to the atrocities of warfare and the role he took as a poet in recording them. He was performing a similar role to modern journalists, embedded with the army. Unlike journalists, however, Owen does not try to remain objective. The change of focus of the second verb conveys feelings of fear, but also guilt at being unable to help the dying man.

Like many other soldiers of the First World War, Owen suffered terribly from shell-shock. The symptoms of shell-shock varied from man to man;

Owen's friend Siegfried Sassoon suffered hallucinations, other soldiers went mute or developed hypersensitivity to loud sounds. Wilfred Owen's shell-shock manifested itself in vivid nightmares:

'In all my dreams, before my helpless sight,
He plunges at me, guttering, choking, drowning'.

After this line Owen moves back into the collective experience,

'the wagon that we flung him in'.

In the last stanza the poet seems almost to lift his head out of the poem and speak directly to his 'friend' and to us, using the simple but powerful device of the second person pronoun, 'you'. The pronoun connects us to Owen's experience and makes us reflect on our attitudes to war and to war propaganda in all its forms.

Owen's description of the dying soldier suggests he certainly felt a helpless sense of responsibility and that, perhaps, this is the reason why he is haunted by the man's death in 'all' his dreams. Owen uses the present continuous participle of 'smothering' as an adjective to describe the dreams. Grammatically this links Owen with the dying soldier.

The poet also experiences feelings of suffocation in his dreams, just as the man had in life.

Owen's sadness and guilt transforms in the last stanza to anger. Anger is projected at people back home who had little understanding of the real conditions on the front line. In particular Owen rages against propagandists who present war as a great adventure, as 'sweet and glorious'. His poem is a powerful corrective to romanticised ideas of war. See, for example, Tennyson's 'The Charge of the Light Brigade' analysed earlier in this book.

Soldiers

Think of an image you would use for recruiting to the British Army. What would you choose? An image of brave, strong, happy, handsome and youthful men in smart uniforms doing exciting, manly work in an exotic location, perhaps? Now look again at the images of the soldiers in the first stanza of 'Dulce et Decorum Est'.

Firstly they have been crippled by the weight of their suffering, 'bent double', 'knock-kneed', they can hardly walk, see or hear; they are 'lame', 'blind' and 'deaf'.

Secondly Owen uses two shocking similes. The soldiers are 'like old beggars', 'coughing like hags'. The comparison to 'beggars' expresses their desperate and shabby state. The simple adjective 'old' shows how the trauma of battle has prematurely aged and enfeebled the men. 'Hags' refers to witch-like, ugly old women, so in this image the men are emasculated. This means having their strength and masculinity taken away.

Thirdly their morale is shot to pieces and they are exhausted: The soldiers 'curse' and 'trudge' and are 'drunk with fatigue'. In other words they are so tired they are almost senseless.

In any situation their state would be awful and pitiable. How much worse though to be so desperately vulnerable so close to the front lines? When they need to be alert to save their lives, the soldiers responses are numbed; out of their minds, they are oblivious to the danger all around them, turning 'their backs' on flares, 'deaf' to the sounds of shells ('five-nines') falling behind them.

The overall impression is of men on their very last legs, at the very end of their tether, almost zombified; the walking dead. If they were to meet German troops now they would be annihilated. The phrase 'distant rest' can mean the support trenches, but metaphorically it also implies death. Owen implies that these men are trudging slowly towards inevitable death.

Owen

Invalided to Craiglockhart hospital in Scotland, Owen was encouraged to turn his nightmares into poetry as part of his therapy for shell-shock. Clearly 'Dulce et Decorum Est' was part of this process.

As we have noted, initially he does not separate himself from the other soldiers; Owen's suffering is the same as the rest of the men. However, officers appeared to have suffered more from mental illness, nervous breakdowns and hysteria than their men. This may have been because they were responsible for looking after soldiers in a situation where this was virtually impossible to do, where death could come suddenly and without warning.

The dying man

As we have seen, the poem starts with the group experience but then zooms in to focus on the death of one representative figure.

Enhanced by Owen's sudden switch to the present tense, the urgent direct speech makes the scene tense and immediate: 'Gas! Gas! Quick boys!'

After the gas explodes the soldier has only moments to fit the respirator that would save his life. In the chaos and confusion he is too slow. The next moment he is 'yelling and stumbling'. His desperation is shown by Owen's choice of the verb 'plunges'. It suggests both the uncontrolled violence of his movement and the idea of water and deep depths.

The physical agony suffered is conveyed through the **SIMILE** of being on fire, 'like a man in fire or lime' and through describing his death as a metaphorical 'drowning'.

The use of three **PRESENT CONTINUOUS PARTICIPLES** (look at the all the words in these two stanzas ending with '-ing') takes us into the scene, as if it is happening before us, and the moment is held for three horrible beats, 'guttering, choking, drowning'.

In the final stanza are further gruesome, hard-hitting images, both visual, his eyes 'writhing' and aural/tactile, 'the blood come gargling', conveying the grotesque suffering of the soldier.

Readers

Owen addresses his audience ironically as 'my friend'. The tone he uses is sardonic, darkly ironic. Originally Owen addressed this poem to a particular person, Jessie Pope, a poet who had written many recruiting poems, including the famous 'Who's for the game?'. In the title, Pope uses a popular euphemism for war, comparing it to sport.

Owen is clearly angry at how writers misrepresented the reality of war, particularly those like Pope who had no direct experience of battle. Hence he is saying if 'you' could have witnessed this horror you would not encourage children to think of war as 'sweet and glorious'.

The choice of the quotation from the Latin poet Horace suggests that writers throughout history have romanticised the experience of war, and Owen's poem is a repudiation of such easy and trite patriotic sentiments.

The 'high zest' he refers to is the enthusiastic relish of war propagandists.

Beyond Pope, Horace and other writers, Owen is addressing all the people back home. Many of the soldiers felt anger at the ignorance of those in England, particularly at the warmongers, those people keenest for the war to continue. Famously Sassoon issued a declaration, published in The Times newspaper, in which he called for the end of what he considered to have become a war of aggression, not liberation:

> *I believe that I may help to destroy the callous complacency with which the majority of those at home regard the contrivance of agonies which they do not, and which they have not sufficient imagination to realize.* Siegfried Sassoon

Owen's use of the pronoun 'you' involves us in the poem, reaching out to pull us into an experience we could otherwise hardly imagine. We too are made to consider our attitudes to war and to war propaganda.

Children

Some of the soldiers who fought in the First World War were just seventeen years old. Most of the millions killed on both sides were young men. Owen himself died in his mid twenties.

Those who signed up had little idea of the reality of trench warfare. They were told of the adventure of a lifetime, as the most glorious of sports; they found blasted landscapes, rats and lice, the rain and mud, no man's land and barbed wire, endless artillery bombardment and gas attacks, body parts in trench walls, mechanised death on a monumental scale.

The children in the poem represent Owen's identification with the soldiers' innocence and the next, easily exploited generation, 'ardent for some desperate glory'.

IMAGERY

What key images do we have in the poem?

The army at the start of the scene, the gas attack, the helmet, the dying man and the images of hell and disease.

We have already analysed how the soldiers and the dying man are presented. Another powerful piece of imagery is the description of the gas dispersing. This is a highly visual, almost cinematic poem. Imagine the poem as a series of frames with specific camera angles and it will help you to understand Owen's technique.

The first stanza is like a long, slow, sweeping, wide-angled shot, showing the whole troop. After the sudden exclamatory shout of 'Gas! Gas!' the camera angles cut much more quickly. The camera spins to find the 'someone' who is the dying man. In the tense moment that follows it is as if the screen goes blank; we know something awful has happened, but we cannot see what it is; we are left only with the disembodied sound of 'yelling out'.

When we do see the man 'floundering' our perspective is initially objective; we are watching him from close by. Next the description switches to what film-makers call a point-of-view shot, where the audience looks through the eyes of a character.

For a moment we are inside the gas mask looking through Owen's eyes:

> 'Dim through the misty pains and thick green light
> as under a green sea, I saw him drowning.'

Picking up the verb 'plunges', the scale of the visual simile of a 'green sea' implies the extraordinary speed with which the gas spreads and the soldier is engulfed and dying.

In addition to the quick switches of perspective, the chaos and confusion of the attack is communicated in a number of other inter-related ways. In particular, perceptions are scrambled and obscured:

- Owen transfers the adjective 'clumsy' from the men to an inanimate object, the 'helmet', so that, momentarily, it as if the helmet is alive.

- A normally very positive word 'ecstasy', is used in a terrifying context, changing its meaning.

- The relief conveyed by the short phrase 'just in time' is immediately countered by the realisation that one man has been too slow.

- 'Someone' implies the panic of not knowing who has been too slow.

- The land seems as if it is the sea; the air is suddenly water.

Look too at verbs. We move from the present tense of 'fitting' to past tense of 'was yelling' and 'I saw' and back into the present with 'plunges'. Past and present are fused; the time between witnessing the gas attack and the reliving it in nightmare collapses.

A later simile implies that the soldiers are in hell; the man's face is 'like a devil's sick of sin'. The idea of sin and sickness is carried forward in the sonically explosive simile, 'obscene as cancer' and in 'vile incurable sores'. Tactile and taste imagery creates a sense of intimate experience, 'bitter...on tongues', further forcing the reader to imagine the experience and recoil in horror from it.

PATTERNS OF SOUND AND SENSE

The insistent alliteration of 'bent' and 'beggars', 'knock-kneed', 'coughing' and 'cursed', coupled with the assonance of 'sacks' and 'hags', 'knock' and 'cough' contribute to what we have already identified as the slowness and heaviness of the opening lines.

TONE is open to interpretation. Anger to one person can sound like sadness to another. However the tone is extremely important in this poem. Initially, with the description of the soldiers, the tone seems neutral, the emotion held back in check; resentment and resignation is constrained. Though he is part of it, Owen is trying to present the scene almost objectively, as if watching from the outside.

The pace and tone shifts violently with the gas attack. A short burst of exclamatory direct speech communicates the shock, panic and alarm:

'Gas! Gas! Quick boys!'

The tone shifts again to appalled horror as Owen watches the soldier dying and modulates into guilt and despair at his inability to help. These inward-turning feelings are concentrated and then projected outwards in the bitter, angry tone of the final stanza. Owen's description is unremitting as he tries to force his readers to feel the man's suffering.

The anger gives way to something colder, more bitter with the ironic, 'my friend'. The verse's repeated sound qualities, such as the repeated pattern of hard, harsh fricatives in 'sick', 'could', 'come', 'corrupted', 'cancer', 'cud' and 'incurable' emphasise this bitterness.

Owen finishes by calling Horace's Latin tag 'the old lie' and again his tone is angry but resolute.

FORM AND STRUCTURE

Metre

Owen's poem is written in **IAMBIC PENTAMETER**, a metre often used in English for poems with serious themes. The lines fall into a roughly iambic pattern, but this metre is often bent, warped and overloaded, as if by the stress of the content.

Look, for example, at the first two lines:

Bent, double, like old beggars under sacks

Ti-TUM ti-   TUM ti-TUM ti-TUM ti-TUM

Knock-kneed, coughing like hags we cursed through sludge

Ti-TUM   TUM-ti   ti-TUM ti-TUM   ti-TUM

Both 'bent and 'knock' could and probably should be stressed. In which case both lines would start TUM TUM and would contain six rather than the regular five beats of a pentameter. Perhaps 'old' should also be stressed. Certainly then, the first two lines are appropriately heavier and slower than a regular iambic pattern. The technical term for this double stress is a **SPONDEE**. And an extra stress in a line is called a **HYPERMETRICAL STRESS**.

Immediately tension is created by extra loading of the first lines of the poem. Often the iambic metre is flexed, put under such strain that it almost breaks down. Look, for instance, at lines such as 'men marched asleep. Many had lost their boots', 'drunk with fatigue; deaf even to the hoots', 'Gas! Gas! Quick boys! – an ecstasy of fumbling', or 'and watch the white eyes writing in his face'.

The first of these lines starts with a spondee, creating an extra stress:

Men marched asleep. Many had lost their boots

TUM-TUM   ti-TUM   TUM-ti ti-TUM ti-TUM

Even if we added an unstressed beat for the emphatic caesura, you can see that the iambic pattern is breaking down here.

The lines 'drunk with fatigue, deaf even to the hoots' and 'and watch the white eyes writhing in his face' are similar in that they have extra beats ('to' in the first line, 'eyes' and 'in' in the second). The **TROCHAIC** pattern of the first one is another deviation from the dominant iambic.

The most startling break down of the iambic pattern is in the line, 'Gas! Gas! Quick, boys!' where two spondees in a row create a short burst of stresses: TUM TUM TUM TUM. The lines often appear to be struggling to keep under control the huge emotions they contain.

Stanzas

As we have seen, there is a tension in the poem between order and fragmentation, between control and degeneration.

For example, the title is the incomplete, broken off first half of a quotation. Many of the lines in the poem are broken down by caesurae; consequently the rhythm is often faltering. Extra, hypermetrical stresses, as in the first two lines, and the intense emotional charge create the impression of a poem almost breaking out of its formal constraints, as if order is breaking down. Mirroring the half quotation title, for instance, the final stanza also ends with a fragmentary half line, 'pro patria mori'.

142

This tension is also conveyed through the ordering pattern of rhyme, working against the irregular, uneven pattern of stanzas. The first stanza is 8 lines, the second has 6 lines, the third 2 and the final stanza has 12.

The two line stanza effectively isolates and connects the dying man and Owen. The dying man lives only in Owen's dreams.

Enjambment and caesurae

Owen sets himself the challenging task of writing a poem that is meant to sound like natural impassioned speech within the constraints of a regular iambic metre and a regular cross-rhyme pattern (ABAB CDCD etc.) Another way to see metre is as a support system, a frame on which the poem's words can be strung.

At times Owen very skilfully uses enjambment and caesura for what is called mimetic effect. By 'mimetic' I mean that the way he says something conveys the experience just as much as what he is saying.

Look at the first two lines:

> 'Bent-double, like old beggars under sacks,
> Knock-kneed, coughing like hags, we cursed through sludge.'

Owen could have written,

> 'we cursed through sludge, bent double like old beggars,
> knock-kneed and coughing like hags'

What's the difference?

The word order, technically called syntax, is very different.

Owen's opening is static, the sentence's subject (the men) and action (cursed) are held back and the reader is left for a while uncertain about who or what is being described.

The effect is to make the verse seem to stagger along – look at those commas – to move with a halting, arrested movement, mimetic of the movement of the soldiers.

CONTEXT

Socio-historical Context

A young man joining up to fight would have had no idea at all what the reality of fighting would be like. The First World War was the first fully mechanised war, with mustard gas, machine guns and tanks. The nature of trench warfare was profoundly different to battle in previous wars, being essentially attritional. The numbers speak for themselves:

- 8 million soldiers were killed.

- Including civilians, about 20 million people died.

- On the first day of the battle of the Somme, 20 thousand men were killed, 60 thousand injured. That's one man dead or injured every second for 24 hours.

- Life expectancy of a junior officer was one month.

Biographical Context

Owen wrote a number of contradictory things about war and poetry. In his preface to his collection of war poems, for instance, he said he was 'above all...not concerned with Poetry', but that "The Poetry is in the Pity'. By this he was seeking to make a distinction between self consciously stylised and elevated grand Poetry and the poetry he was writing, which was more grounded in reality, more concerned with truth than style.

Owen also called himself a 'conscientious objector with a very seared conscience'. In other words he felt deeply ambivalent about the war and his role in it. There was a powerful tension in his character between different conceptions of himself. On the one side was the Christian, poetic self - sensitive, compassionate and romantic, in love with the works of Romantic poets, such as Keats and Shelley. On the other side was the soldierly self: disciplined, manly, ordered, heroic, stoical.

Much of Owen's finest poetry springs from this internal conflict. You might, for instance, wish to look up 'Strange Meeting' in which Owen's double nature is most explicit.

Visual

Compare Owen's poem to the famous painting 'Gassed' by John Singer Sargent. Which piece of art do you think is more powerful? Why?

THE POEM CRUNCHED

Highlight these words in each line and then make the background words disappear

Before reading our list, have a go at crunching the poem. This means reducing each line to just one word. Think carefully about which word you think is the most important one in each line, write this down and then compare.

Beggars – hags - haunting – rest- asleep – blind – deaf - Five-Nines – gas – clumsy – someone – fire – green – sea – dreams – drowning – smothering – flung – writhing – sin – blood – obscene – incurable – friend – children – lie - mori

KEY REVISION

Themes

- not an anti-war poem, but anti-war propaganda and the romanticising of war

- the suffering of the ordinary soldiers

- the psychological impact of war

Language

- a cinematic quality to the writing

- makes the unfamiliar familiar, using vivid imagery, drawing on all the senses

- powerful, vivid visual imagery enhanced by sonic effects, like the soundtrack of a film

- taste and touch evoked to create a sense of movement and action

- direct speech to help take us into the scene

- rhetorical, making an argument

Form and structure

- Tension runs through the poem between opposing forces of order and degeneration.

- The form is under stress; the iambic pentameter almost breaks down.

- While the regular rhyme scheme sustains control, the irregular stanza form generates a sense of disorder and fragmentation.

Contexts

- Owen's best poetry expressed a conflict between his compassion for the suffering of he soldiers and his conviction that the war was necessary.

- He was part of a generation of poets acting as witnesses and reporters whose descriptions of the horror fundamentally shaped our understanding of trench warfare.

True or false? Wilfred Owen was killed only one week before the end of WW1.

rage rage
against
the
dying of the light

Do Not Go Gentle Into That Good Night

Do not go gentle into that good night,
Old age should burn and rave at close of day;
Rage, rage against the dying of the light.

Though wise men at their end know dark is right,
Because their words had forked no lightning they
Do not go gentle into that good night.

Good men, the last wave by, crying how bright
Their frail deeds might have danced in a green bay,
Rage, rage against the dying of the light.

Wild men who caught and sang the sun in flight,
And learn, too late, they grieved it on its way,
Do not go gentle into that good night.

Grave men, near death, who see with blinding sight
Blind eyes could blaze like meteors and be gay,
Rage, rage against the dying of the light.

And you, my father, there on that sad height,
Curse, bless, me now with your fierce tears, I pray.
Do not go gentle into that good night.
Rage, rage against the dying of the light.

Dylan Thomas (1951)

INTRODUCTION

According to the Chambers Dictionary, **EUPHEMISM** is 'a figure of rhetoric by which an unpleasant or offensive thing is designated by a milder term'. We tend to find euphemistic language is used around subjects which are in some way 'untouchable', or taboo. It is usually a means of evading, or glossing over, or just making light of realities that are hard to face directly.

From time to time my mother will say something like 'Of course it's very sad, she lost her husband five years ago', to which I invariably reply 'Oh dear, has she found him yet?' Naturally the older we get, the more attractive euphemistic language around death becomes. There are many euphemistic terms for death, such as 'passed away', 'at rest' and 'kicked the bucket'.

Rather like dead metaphor (for example, 'a chair leg'), euphemistic language often creeps by us unnoticed. But if you listen out for it you will find it is widely used. You hear genocide referred to on the news as 'ethnic cleansing', and the inadvertent killing of civilians called 'collateral damage', or elderly relatives announcing that they are going to 'spend a penny'.

But what possible use could a poet make of euphemism? Isn't it part of a poet's job to bring us closer to reality, not evade it, gloss over it, or distance us from it?

Dylan Thomas makes euphemistic language central to this poem. We will see that it enables him to achieve the emotional distance required to deal with an ultra taboo subject. But at the same time, something miraculous occurs; that same language also uncannily allows the reader closer to the reality he is describing. We'll explore this in the section on imagery.

The poem is not just about death, it is about the impending death of the poet's father. This is what makes it really taboo - it is addressed to the poet's living father, regarding his impending death. In fact he lived for over a year longer. Imagine receiving a poem like that in the post!

CHARACTERS

Narrator

Thomas' poem is written in the first person, but the 'I' only comes in during the final stanza, when we realise that the poet has been addressing the poem specifically to his dying father: 'And you, my father, there on the sad height'. Having started with a seemingly generalised public imperative to people in old age, the poem circles towards this deeply personal finale.

The withholding of the personal voice makes its eventual appearance in the poem more dramatic and powerful.

Before the poet and his father come into it, the poem concerns itself with character types: wise men, good men, wild men, grave men, and the different reasons why they don't go quietly to their deaths. These types give Thomas examples by which to measure the success of his father's life, and implicitly his own.

What do we learn of the characters of father and son? Well the son, the poet, is using this difficult villanelle form, its repeat lines and formality, to wrestle strong and potentially overwhelming emotions under control. That's my impression. But when we also know that the father was a teacher of English and lover of literature, we have a sense of a son wanting to please his father with an unassailably great poem, to prove his poetic mastery once and for all.

Perhaps even to show off a bit, "Look dad! Look what I've made!"

And of course in the world of the poem, the father's death, though impending, is always in the future, has never happened. So there is an element of the poet's wish-fulfilment. But also there is the sense of the poet bringing on the father's death – reading the poem you would have the impression the father's death was imminent. In reality he lived another year.

Father

Thomas' father was an atheist, so that for him his impending death was very definitely the 'end'. The poem never contradicts this view; all the way through, death is described as the end. However it is the first use of the words 'my father' which, ironically given this father's atheism, alerts us to some spiritual yearning in the poet.

The little harmonic note of meaning of 'priest' that comes with the word 'father' is confirmed in the next line, where the poet moves for the first time from a tone of command to one of supplication:

> *'Curse, bless, me now with your fierce tears, I pray.'*

The Verbs used by the narrator are:

- Do not go

- rage

- dying.

The repeat lines are **IMPERATIVES**, commands , instructions.

In the second line we are told old age should 'burn' and 'rave'.

Other Men

The verbs associated with the old men, wise men and the other character types are:

know; had forked; crying; danced; caught; sang; learn; grieved; see; blaze; be.

The instructions are turned then to the poet's father: curse; bless.

Then the repeat lines return at the end and are now directed in all their universality and power at the poet's dying father.

But first the weight of the whole poem and its tone of command and instruction is modulated by the poet's only verb: I pray.

IMAGERY

Objects in the poem: night, light, men, dark, words, lightning, wave, deeds, bay, sun, eyes, meteors, father, height, tears.

We've talked earlier about euphemistic language. Now I want to analyse how it functions in this poem. The first thing to note is that it always appears as a line ending. The two repeat lines or refrains both end with key euphemistic imagery; 'that good night' and 'the dying of the light'. The two other examples are end of line 2 'at close of day' and end line 16 'on the sad height'.

'At close of day' ties in with the age old idea of death as a kind of sleep, e.g. 'And our little life is rounded with a sleep' (from 'The Tempest'). Its implication of sunset and then darkness ties in with the rest of the poem's imagery of light for life, dark for death:

- 'lightning'

- 'bright' waves

- 'the sun'

- 'blaze like meteors'

What makes this imagery of light different and startling is that it is in the context of people realising late in life how much more light they could have had, how much more fully they could have lived, and being angry, raging about that fact.

Line 16 '...on the sad height' uses the **METAPHOR** of life as an ascent: old age is a plateau reached near the top, where the ageing process all but ceases; there is a creeping towards death, but there really is nowhere else to go, except the slightly higher summit which is death. Time is passing, but less is happening. The phrase gives us a sense of time for reflection, perhaps wisdom, but no more action.

As remarked earlier, euphemism is usually used to soften hard reality. It does so here too. As a result of the distancing euphemisms we don't feel mawkishly close to the death-bed, or feel that the poet is being self-indulgently emotional. But the use of this kind of language in both refrains has a strange effect. The repetition gives the reader a sense of knocking on the doors of the exact meaning and imagery of each euphemism, trying to open it up, trying to get in. The poem won't permit us to let the euphemism glide by and have a numbing or pacifying effect. Instead it wakes up to its own effects through the course of the poem.

Each time a line is resurrected we become more aware of it, and it more directly and intensely suggests death.

PATTERNS OF SOUNDS AND SENSE

The rhyme scheme is aba aba aba aba aba abaa. Being on only two rhymes makes the poem a closed form. This is accentuated by the two repeat lines, which each occur four times in the poem.

In tension with this sealed closedness is the simultaneously expansive and commanding note struck by the repeat lines. Because they have to bear being repeated each line, they need to be open in the sense that they can bear different weights and loads of meaning from the lines around them as the poem progresses.

They sound rather cool and almost detached when we first hear them, but by the end those same lines are freighted up with grief and desperation.

The poet uses the technique of two verbs linked by 'and' to create a feeling of activity:

- 'burn and rave'

- 'caught and sang'.

This sense of poise and balance echoes the idea of hovering between life and death.

The first line is an arresting and unusual construction: 'Do not' sets the tone as formal and commanding from the off, and 'gentle' where we expect 'gently' brings the reader's mind to a slight pause and jarring appropriate for what follows – the poem's word order is at times used to slow the reader; reading the poem is intentionally a **SYNTACTICALLY** bumpy ride.

FORM AND STRUCTURE

Thomas' poem is a **VILLANELLE**. This is a nineteen line poem with two rhymes, the second lines of each stanza on one rhyme, all the rest on the other. The first and third lines of the poem repeat alternately as the third lines in subsequent stanzas, and becoming the very last two lines of the poem.

In a great villanelle like this, the repeated lines build in resonance and power as the poem progresses, and they blend in seamlessly with the surrounding lines. They make the poem's movement circling and wavelike rather than flat and linear. Their statement and restatement gives a feeling of the provisional, but also can, as here, be used to capture desperation, anxiety and enclosure.

CONTEXTS

Dylan Thomas wrote the poem in the Summer/Autumn of 1951. His father died in December 1952. Dylan Thomas's sister died of cancer in Bombay in April 1953. Dylan Thomas himself died in November 1953, aged 39 years.

Thomas embraced rhyme and often difficult poetic forms, at a time when many '**MODERNIST**' writers were writing free verse. One of these writers, Kingsley Amis, famously jibed about Thomas 'spewing words like beer'. Though he only ever wrote in English, his mother and father both knew the Welsh language. Perhaps the strict forms are to some extent a nod to the Welsh Bardic tradition, famous for its exacting technical rigours.

THE POEM CRUNCHED

Obviously, this process will always be a personal one. This is just one possibility. Do it yourself and see where we agree and disagree. What have you spotted that I have not?

> *Night – age – rage -dark - lightning – gentle – wave – deeds – dying – sun – grieved – good – blinding Blaze – light – father – bless – gentle - rage*

KEY REVISION

Themes

- differing attitudes to life and death
- regrets and the relationship between father and son
- Atheism and Religion

Language

- heightened, intensely emotional pitch
- strong, insistent rhymes
- repetition building to rhetorical effect
- euphemism
- distance, then first person coming in at last stanza, 'my', 'I'

Form and Structure

- villanelle, a very difficult, closed form
- two rhymes only
- strong but open repeat lines (able to function through changing contexts)

Contexts

- Thomas wrote in the era of Modernism, yet he renews and reinvigorates old forms.

- He rhymes brilliantly and naturally while many around moved over to free verse.

- His poetry remains popular and readable.

True or false? Dylan Thomas's poetry was described by the satirical novelist, Kingsley Amis, as "spewing words like beer".

Glossary

- **ADJECTIVE** - a describing word, that gives more information about a noun.

- **ALLITERATION** - the repetition of sounds in nearby words, most often involving the initial consonants of words (eg slippery snake).

- **ANTITHESIS** - the contrast or opposition of ideas eg "you are the enemy I killed, my friend"(Wilfred Owen).

- **ARCHETYPAL** - an original model or type after which other similar things are patterned.

- **ASSONANCE** - the repetition of vowel sounds in a line or series of lines. Assonance often affects pace eg "strong gongs groaning as the guns boom far" (Chesterton).

- **BALLADS** - poems that tells a story similar to a folk tale or legend and often with a repeated refrain.

- **BLANK VERSE** - is poetry that is written in unrhymed iambic pentameter.

- **CAESURA** - a pause in a line of verse created by sense or natural speech rhythm rather than meter.

- **CONCEIT** - sets up an analogy between some spiritual qualities and an object in the physical world (such as the flea in John Donne's poem). It becomes a form of extended metaphor.

- **DIMETER** - a line of two iambic feet.

- **DRAMATIC MONOLOGUE** - one person, who is definitely not the poet, utters the speech that makes up the whole of the poem.

- **ELEGY** - since the Renaissance usually a formal lament for the death of a particular person.

- **ELLIPSIS** - the omission from a sentence or poem of one or more words that would complete or clarify the poem.

- **END STOP** - a line break that coincides with the end of the sentence (vs. a run-on line; compare enjambment).

- **ENJAMBMENT** - from the French word for "to straddle" is the continuation of a sentence from one line or couplet into the next.

- **EUPHEMISM** - a harmless word that replaces an offensive or suggestive one - "passed away" for death.

- **EXTENDED METAPHORS** - detailed and complex metaphors that extend over a long section of a poem - the flea in Donne's poem.

- **FEMININE AND MASCULINE RHYME** - a masculine rhyme has a single-syllable rhyme (time/rhyme) at the very end of a line, whereas a feminine rhyme means more than one syllable is rhymed at the end of a line (pleasure/measure).

- **FRAME NARRATOR** - provides a personal perspective at the start and close of the poem.

- **HYPERBOLE** - exaggeration for poetic effect.

- **IMAGERY** - an object that is not really there is used in order to create a comparison between one that is, evoking a more meaningful visual experience for the reader.

- **IAMBIC** - (ti-TUM) a foot of two syllables, the first unstressed or short, and the second long or stressed.

- **IAMBIC TETRAMETER** - a line consisting of four iambic feet.

- **LYRIC POEMS** - address the reader directly, portraying his or her own feeling, state of mind, or perceptions.

- **METAPHOR** - one term is applied to another to suggest a resemblance - "his eyes blazed" suggests his eyes were like fire.

- **METER** - the number of syllables in each line and the arrangement of those syllables as long or short, accented or unaccented.

- **MOTIF** - a repetition of an idea, or a line (refrain) or a situation that deliberately connects a poem to an associated meaning.

- **NARRATOR** - the voice in a poem which presents a particular point of view, not to be confused with the author.

- **OCTAVE** - a rhythmic group of eight lines of poetry.

- **ONOMATOPOEIA** -is a type of word that sounds like the thing it is describing.

- **OXYMORON** - a figure of speech that combines two apparently contradictory words eg bitter-sweet.

- **PATHETIC FALLACY** - is the treatment of inanimate objects as if they had human feelings, thought, or sensations eg "the cruel sea".

- **PENTAMETER** - a line of verse with five metrical feet.

- **PLOSIVE ALLITERATION** - an repetition of a consonantal sound in the formation of which the passage of air is completely blocked, such as 'p', 'b', 't'.

- **QUATRAIN POETRY** - is a stanza or poem of four lines. Lines 2 and 4 must rhyme. Lines 1 and 3 may or may not rhyme.

- **REFRAIN** - repeating a line eg "half a league, half a league, half a league onward....." (Tennyson).

- **SESTET** - varieties of six line poems (or part of poems, such as the closing part of a sonnet) whose rhyme forms can differ.

- **SIBILANCE** - producing a hissing sound like that of (s) or (sh).

- **STANZA** - a grouping of two or more lines set off by a space, that usually has a set pattern of meter and rhyme. The stanza in poetry functions like a paragraph in prose, where related thoughts are grouped into units.

- **STASIS** - a form of balance or equilibrium where opposing forces or meanings cancel each other out.

- **SYMBOL** - symbols are messages within a word that must be analysed to discover their meaning.

- **SYNESTHESIA** - figurative expression of the perception of one sense in terms of another eg"And the hapless Soldier's sigh / Runs in blood down Palace walls." (William Blake)

- **SYNTAX** - the arrangement of words in a sentence.

- **TRIMETER** - a line of three iambic feet.

- **TROCHEE** - (TUM-ti) a metrical foot consisting of a stressed or long syllable followed by an unstressed or short syllable.

- **VERB** - that in syntax conveys an action (bring,read, walk, run, learn), an occurrence (happen, become), or a state of being (be, exist, stand).

- **VILLANNELLE** - the very specific repetition of two lines, with two other alternating rhymed lines.

- **VOLTA** - a change in tone often signalled by "but"' "yet" or "and yet", often found in the last two lines of a sonnet eg "And yet, by heaven, I think my love as rare/ As any she belied with false compare." (Shakespeare, sonnet 130)

- **SUBLIME** - the extremes of awe, beauty or terror, often located for romantic writers in wild landscapes.

Source (adapted) from www.english.cam.ac.uk

Postscript

Neil Bowen has been teaching English for 15 years, working in both the state and independent sectors. Currently he is Head of English at Wells Cathedral School in Somerset. He has written many articles on English Literature and a number of popular teaching resources for 'A' level. Recently he has started a Masters Degree in Literature and Teaching at Cambridge University.

Neil created and runs the literature website, peripeteia.web.com.

An award winning poet, Matthew Curry has written many articles and resources on poets, including Emily Dickinson, W.B. Yeats and Wilfred Owen. 'In Galloway', Matthew's walking guide with accompanying poems, was a Hay Festival Book of the Year in 2012.

An Irish English teacher with a first class degree in Engineering and a Masters degree in American Literature, Michael Meally is head of 'A' level English at Wells Cathedral School, Somerset.

Currently a Pastoral Head of Year 11, Sally Rowley is a highly experienced teacher of GCSE English who has also been an examiner for English Literature at 'A' level.